November

Dear Janice,

I trust that you will find ~~the~~ information contained in this book useful.

In Christ's Love,

Joel

THE ONE TRUE CHURCH

A Biblical Perspective on Catholic Tradition and History

JOE WELLER

The One True Church
A Biblical Perspective on Catholic Tradition and History
by Joe Weller

Printed in the United States of America.

Edited by Xulon Press

ISBN 9781498431125

"The nature of this manuscript, being written in stages over thirty years, requires the author to make certain disclaimers. Detailed reference sources are not always indicated because of the time that has lapsed. Every effort has been made to identify the general publications used for those various comments throughout the text. I have chosen a personal style of writing in an attempt to make this material straightforward and understandable. A traditional biblical dating system was chosen because of the nature of the general audience."

Unless otherwise indicated, Scripture quotations taken from The New American Catholic Bible, Nihil Obstat:Stephen J. Hardegen, O.F.M., S.S.L., Imprimatur:Patrick Cardinal O'Boyle, D.D. Archbishop of Washington.

www.xulonpress.com

Dedication

To Carol, my true love, my partner in life, and my loyal wife of forty-four years. Thank you for your extraordinary patience and support during my thirty-plus year spiritual journey.

Table of Contents

I

Prologue

Dear Friend,

The Bible tells us that all are sinners in need of a Savior. Sin, therefore, does not discriminate between different Christians and their religious institutions or denominations. The content of this book represents over thirty years of personal experience, research, observation, study, and prayer in an effort to demonstrate through the Bible, and through history, that The One True Church is not an institutional church or a specific religious denomination but rather all true believers who belong to the Body of Christ throughout the ages. An effort has been made to share this truth by giving a clear biblical presentation that includes God's plan of salvation as a resource to those whom the Holy Spirit might seek, regardless of their religious affiliation or station in life.

What is it that we must do to be a part of this spiritual "Body of Christ?"

I trust that you will find *The One True Church* helpful in your search for God's truth. This book was written for Catholics and non-Catholics alike who are seeking a deeper understanding of Catholic history and traditions from a biblical perspective. Over the centuries the Catholic Church has evolved into a complex religious organization of beliefs, rules, rituals, and requirements described as "speculative and mystical theology," by a leading Catholic apologist, who says that most Catholics do not fully understand and can't explain their religion to others. This book can be a useful resource for these individuals and others who have an interest in understanding what Catholics teach and what Protestants believe, regardless of their religious backgrounds.

As a practicing Catholic for the first thirty-eight years of my life, I did not write this book to offend Catholics or in an attempt to elevate any other Christian institution, denomination, or church to a superior spiritual position. This book was not written as a document attempting to witness to Catholics or anyone else but rather as a resource for those seeking knowledge about the evolution of Christianity. It is clear from the Bible that all individuals, whether Catholic or non-Catholic, are justified or saved only by the intercession of the Holy Spirit and the grace of God, not by any man's human effort at trying to convince others as to what they should believe. This book represents the author's sincere efforts to objectively evaluate certain traditions and beliefs of the church from a historical and biblical perspective.

It is my sincere desire that this work would encourage the reader to do their own research and study the spiritual treasures locked in the pages of Holy Scripture and come to their own conclusion about who embodies The One True Church.

It's all about Him,
Joe Weller
March 2015

Preface

Growing up Catholic in the Bible Belt was a challenging experience. My hometown was situated almost in the center of the geographical area of the United States often referred to as the Bible Belt. While exact lines of demarcation do not exist for the Bible Belt, it is generally considered to cover much of the thirteen-state area stretching from Texas in the Southwest, north to Oklahoma and Missouri, east to Kentucky and Virginia, and finally south to central Florida, including the states of Arkansas, Alabama, Georgia, Louisiana, Tennessee, South Carolina, and North Carolina. This area was characterized by very high church attendance, dominated by Evangelical Protestants.

My home turf as a child was a working-class neighborhood located within walking distance of the Tennessee-Georgia state line. Only two Catholic families, including ours, lived in the neighborhood. Conscientious parents made it a point to see that we were at Mass on Sundays and Holy Days. The Catholic Church required all Catholic children to attend Catholic school, so my four brothers, my sister, and I attended

Catholic parochial school for the majority of our education from the first grade through high school graduation. The parochial school that we attended was the same school that my father and his mother before him had attended.

Our lives were often punctuated by events that would be remembered for a lifetime and that had the effect of solidifying our attitudes about religion and justice. One such event was a Ku Klux Klan rally at a lumberyard near our house in the mid-1950s. As an object lesson, our mother allowed two of my brothers and me, under the supervision of our oldest brother, who was in high school at the time, to observe this KKK rally at a safe distance. Her only admonition was, "Tell no one that you are a Catholic." The messages that resonated from the hooded men behind the megaphone were those of hatred, bigotry, and ignorance, yet the key speaker held a big red Bible in his hand and often invoked the name of God. While holding the Bible, he spewed his venom of hatred for blacks, Jews, and Catholics. I realized from that day forward that I was as much a minority as blacks or Jews in this area of the country. I knew what they were doing was morally wrong, so this reinforced the validity of my Catholic faith. The Catholic Church had taught me that I was a member of The One True Church, and this event, along with numerous other encounters with the Protestant majority reaffirmed the moral superiority of the Catholic Church in my impressionable young mind. It would be some thirty years later that I would fully realize that the KKK's interpretation of the Bible and God's will was a perversion of Christianity and had no place in true Bible-based Christianity.

My twelve years' experience at Catholic school was very positive as I learned from the nuns and priests the Catholic Church's teachings on church doctrines along with reading, writing, and arithmetic. My teachers were dedicated people who strove to teach basic education and to convey to the students what they had been taught by the Catholic Church on matters of faith and morals. My Catholic school education and the discipline attained there served me well over the years. I lettered in three sports in high school, and our small school often defeated schools with much larger athletic programs. At one football game, as we left the field at half-time, I remember hearing several fans in the stands calling us "dirty papists," and one man actually threw a cup of hot coffee at us. We went back out in the second half of the game, unfazed, and won the game. My logic was that God must be with us. Experiences like this did nothing to detract from my feeling of belonging to The One True Church.

Being raised as a Catholic in the Bible Belt in the 1950s brought with it a form of religious persecution from the majority Protestant population that was overt, and at times even covert. While there is still some of this residual bias today, there appears to be more harmony among Protestants and Catholics as common ground has been found on issues like abortion and family values that the rest of society as a whole has depreciated.

This development is an encouraging sign that has created some limited dialogue between Catholics and Protestants on subjects that both sides can agree on. Interestingly, over the years some of my Protestant friends from heavy Catholic areas like Boston and Mexico shared with me that they experienced some of the same type of prejudice that I did but in reverse.

I continued to attend Mass and to receive the sacraments all through my college days, and when I went out in the work force after graduation from college, my Catholic faith was an important part of my life. Then I met my wife of forty-four years. We were married in her Baptist church in East Texas with a Catholic priest and a Baptist minister co-celebrating the service. Our children were baptized Catholics, and my wife faithfully attended mass with me for thirteen years. My wife also taught a Sunday school class for a short period in our local parish church and discussed becoming a Catholic with our priest, but this came to an impasse on the Catholic Church's teachings about Mary. Our local parish priest told my wife that she could not convert to Catholicism if she did not believe all of the Catholic doctrines about Mary.

My wife was beginning to feel that she needed to reconnect with her childhood faith. Our local parish priest strongly suggested that I should not object to my wife attending her own church. We continued to attend mass together on Sunday mornings, and my wife attended a community church service on Sunday evenings. Since she had to drive some distance at night in Southern California, I decided it would be safer if I went with her. I liked the preacher, so it was a real educational experience for me comparing the content of the two church services each Sunday.

After some months into this routine my daughter came home from Confraternity of Christian Doctrine (CCD) classes one day and wanted to know why she had to kneel in front of a statue of the Blessed Virgin, light a candle, and say a prayer to Mary. I told her to do whatever the CCD teacher told her to do. I then left on a two-week business trip but was troubled by the trite response I had given my daughter. This realization began my two-year journey for an appropriate answer to my daughter's question. In a search for truth, I began to read everything I could get my hands on about my Church's history and her teachings. It was an all-consuming quest to learn the truth and to validate the faith and teachings that I loved and had been taught at our parochial school and had practiced devoutly at our local parish church as a young boy.

After two years of intense study I concluded that my Catholic education, while very positive at the time, had taught me only part of the real story of the evolution of the Roman Catholic Church. Events such as the Inquisition were avoided. Many of the doctrines that I was taught were from the days of the apostles actually had been introduced later in history. I am convinced, however, that the nuns and priests' intentions were honorable, but they were also instructed by a centuries-old religious system that had, over time, acquired many church traditions that were not based on Scripture.

While I loved my family and friends in the Catholic Church, and all the rituals of Catholicism, I decided to leave the Catholic Church at thirty-eight years old because I realized that my relationship with Jesus Christ, from a biblical perspective, was more important than my attachment to the Catholic Church or to any institutional church. I had intellectually loved the Lord, but now my heart and my life were changed forever. I was baptized at Grace Community Church, Sun Valley, California, on November 10, 1983.

Once I made the decision to leave the Catholic Church, I felt I should write a letter with the reasons that I was leaving and send it to family members. I wanted them to realize that my decision was not a whim but a thoughtful decision made over time and after a great deal of research and prayer. The letter was nine pages long and detailed the doctrinal differences that I believed I had found while comparing Catholic teaching with biblical truth. It was that letter that was the impetus for writing this book. Reflecting on my early life as a persecuted Catholic, I began to realize how strong a Catholic I had become because of that, and how the early Apostolic Church had also grown strong while under persecution. I believe that my decision to leave Catholicism was from God. I also realized how difficult it is for practicing Catholics raised in the Bible belt to make such a decision to leave the church of their birth.

My heart goes out to the wonderful Catholic people who find themselves in a religious system that offers many wonderful family values, beautiful rituals, and support systems but is flawed in a number of its teachings when compared with the Bible. When the apostle Paul was writing to the church in Corinth, he could easily have also been writing to the Catholic Church, and many other churches of our day, when he wrote, "*For if one comes and preaches another Jesus whom we have not preached, or you receive a different spirit which you have not received, or a different gospel which you have not accepted, you bear this beautifully*" (2 Corinthians 11:4). Many Catholics and non-Catholics alike have been exposed to a different Jesus than the Jesus of the Bible, and many spend their entire lives without knowing the difference.

Many Catholics live exemplary lives of service to their fellow man that would put some evangelicals to shame. Catholic schools, hospitals, and charities make a significant positive contribution to society as a whole. While these are all worthy activities from a social point of view, God's justification economy only recognizes those good works that are the fruit of righteousness, the result of saving faith. All the good works of man done for the best intentions, whether one is a Catholic or non-Catholic, do not save man's soul from destruction.

The One True Church has been a thirty-year labor of love to present the truth of the Word of God to those individuals who want to know what the Catholic Church believes and teaches and how these doctrines compare to God's divinely inspired Word in the Bible from a layman's perspective. Over the years this document has grown from the original nine-page letter to a book as I have grown spiritually and as the Catholic Church has continued to evolve. All Bible quotes and references used in *The One True Church*, if not otherwise noted, are taken directly from the New American Catholic Bible (Imprimatur: Patrick Cardinal O'Boyle). My wife gave me this Bible as a gift in the late 1970s.

The Roman Catholic Church has historically taught that no one can find salvation outside the Catholic Church. Pope John Paul XXIII (1958–1963) said, "Into this fold of Jesus Christ no one can enter if not under the guidance of the Sovereign Pontiff." Evangelical Protestants, on the other hand, believe that anyone can be saved by a simple child-like faith in Jesus Christ as presented in God's Word in the Bible. We must repent of our sins and believe in the Jesus Christ of the Scriptures. This heart-changing experience has nothing to do with infant baptism, joining a church denomination, saying a certain prayer, or walking down a church aisle. Instead, it is a personal relationship with Jesus Christ, whereby our very nature is changed, and we begin to live the Good News of the gospel message: "*For if you confess with your lips that Jesus is Lord, and believe in your heart that God raised Him from the dead you will be saved. Faith in the heart leads to justification, confession on the lips to Salvation.*

. . . *Everyone who calls on the name of the Lord will be saved*" (Romans 10:9–10, 13).

Believers have a serious responsibility to lovingly share God's Gospel message of repentance and salvation with anyone God brings into their lives who may not possess a saving faith in Jesus Christ. Many professing Christians do not know the Good News of God's plan of salvation through His Son Jesus Christ. The believer's responsibility is one of true agape love, not to be prideful that they know something that others do not. God must seek the sinner before the sinner can seek God, so the believer's role as a true disciple of Christ is to serve the Holy Spirit in this process by being available to share His Word.

My prayer is that those who read, *The One True Church* will be prompted to do their own study of God's Word so that they might experience God's love, truth, and saving faith first hand and not place their hope for salvation in the powerless doctrines and traditions of men.

Note: The nature of this manuscript, written in stages over thirty years, requires the author to make certain disclaimers. Detailed reference sources are not always indicated because of the time that has lapsed. Every effort has been made to identify the general publications used for those various comments throughout the text. I have chosen a personal style of writing in an attempt to make this material straightforward and understandable. A traditional biblical dating system was chosen because of the nature of the general audience.

II

Introduction

Many religions, religious movements, and cults have at one time or another declared themselves the one true church. The Mormons claim that they are the only true church on earth. Jehovah's Witnesses claim, "The Watch Tower Bible and Tract Society are the one and only channel which the Lord used in dispensing his truth continually since the beginning of the harvest period." World religions like Hinduism, Buddhism, Islam, and Judaism also claim that they are the true representatives of God on earth.

Several denominations that claim to believe in the first century Christian creeds: the Trinity, virgin birth, the Resurrection, and the deity of Christ, also claim to be the one true church. This would include the Seventh-day Adventists, who observe Saturday for worship and place a heavy emphasis on health and diet; the Church of Christ, which claims, "There is one church! There is one kingdom of God and this is it"; and the Roman Catholic Church. The Roman

Catholic Church believes that she is The One True Church that was established by Christ when He said in Matthew 16:18, "... *thou art Peter, and upon this rock I will build my church; and the gates of hell shall not prevail against it*." The Catholic Church believes that the pope is directly descended from Peter.

Most people who call themselves Christians would, of course, most likely discount the validity of Hinduism, Buddhism, Islam, Mormonism, and Judaism, but it gets somewhat confusing after that preliminary judgment. Clearly the largest group that call themselves Christian and believes that they are *The One True Church* is the Roman Catholic Church, with some 1.1 billion members worldwide (Pew Research, 2010). In 1302, Pope Boniface VIII (1294–1303) made the claim "We declare it to be altogether necessary to salvation that every human creature should be subject to the Roman Pontiff." This claim has been perpetuated throughout the ages. In 1442, Pope Eugene IV wrote:

> The most Holy Roman Church firmly believes, professes and preaches that none of those existing outside the Catholic Church, not only pagans, but also Jews and heretics and schismatics, can have a share in life eternal; but that they will go into the eternal fire which was prepared for the devil and his angels

> (Matthew 25:41), unless before death they are joined with Her; and that so important is the unity of this ecclesiastical body that only those remaining within this unity can profit by the sacraments of the Church unto salvation, and they alone can receive an eternal recompense for their fasts, their almsgiving, their other works of Christian piety and the duties of a Christian soldier. No one, let his almsgiving be as great as it may, no one, even if he pour out his blood for the Name of Christ, can be saved, unless he remain within the bosom and unity of the Catholic Church (11th Session of the Council of Florence).

Vatican II's *Decree on Ecumenism*

In 1856, Pope Pius IX wrote, "Outside of the Church (Roman Catholic), nobody can hope for life or salvation unless he is excused through ignorance beyond his control" (*Singulari Quidem*). In 1928, Pope Pius XI wrote, "The Catholic church alone is keeping the true worship. This is the font of truth, this is the house of faith, this is the temple of God; if any man enter not here, or if any man go forth from it, he is a stranger to the hope of life and salvation" (*Mortalium Animos*). In 1963, Pope John XXIII said, "Into this fold of Jesus Christ no one can enter if not under the guidance of the Sovereign Pontiff." In the early 1960s, Vatican II's *Decree on Ecumenism* tried to soften the harsh language against Protestantism and attempted to create a dialogue with its "separated brethren" but in no way abandoned its belief that the Roman Catholic Church was The One True Church. "For it is only through Christ's Catholic Church, which is 'the all-embracing means of salvation' that they (separated brethren) can benefit from the means of salvation." *(Decree on Ecumenism*, Chapter I, last paragraph, and section 3). The One True Church doctrine of the Roman Catholic Church is the "glue" that holds together all of the dogmas, doctrines, rituals, rules, and traditions of Catholicism.

The Eternal Word Television Network—EWTN

Many Catholics are unaware of these historical and official Papal Encyclicals and Proclamations and would likely have the view that anyone that has a Christian baptism, and believes in Jesus Christ could be saved. The Eternal Word Television Network (EWTN), founded in 1981 as the evangelical arm of Catholicism in the United States, has attempted to soften the hard line position of numerous popes over the centuries by trying to reformulate the strict position of the Vatican, to be more inclusive regarding other Christians as an evangelical out-reach to their viewers.

Catholic Belief: A Short and Simple Exposition of Catholic Doctrine, published in 1884, by Father Joseph Di Bruno, is a key resource recommended by EWTN to those viewers who question the historical position of the church on the doctrine that "Outside the Church there is no salvation." Father Di Bruno gives a rather ambiguous, highly conditional—but clearly an attempt to be more inclusive—explanation of his view of the Catholic Church position on Protestant salvation. Father Di Bruno writes:

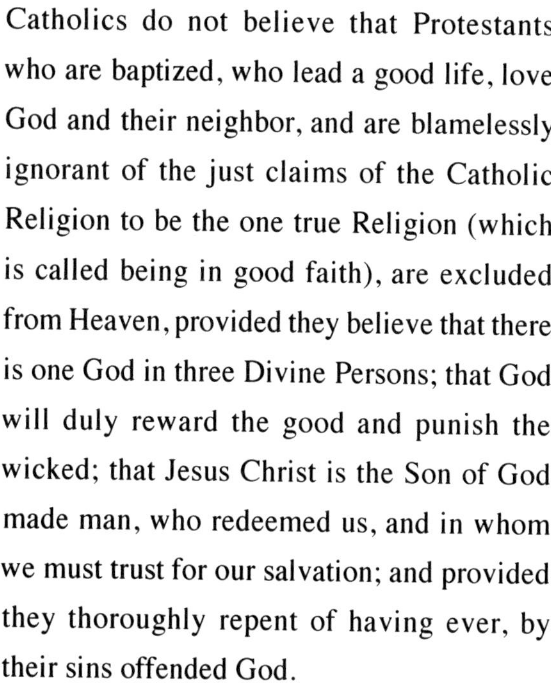

> Catholics do not believe that Protestants who are baptized, who lead a good life, love God and their neighbor, and are blamelessly ignorant of the just claims of the Catholic Religion to be the one true Religion (which is called being in good faith), are excluded from Heaven, provided they believe that there is one God in three Divine Persons; that God will duly reward the good and punish the wicked; that Jesus Christ is the Son of God made man, who redeemed us, and in whom we must trust for our salvation; and provided they thoroughly repent of having ever, by their sins offended God.

Father Di Bruno continues:

> Catholics hold that Protestants who have these dispositions, and who have no suspicion of their religion being false, and no means to discover, or fail in their honest endeavors to discover, the true Religion, and who are so disposed in their heart that they would at any cost embrace the Roman Catholic Religion if they knew it to be the true one, are Catholics in spirit and in some sense within the Catholic Church, without themselves knowing it. She holds that these Christians belong to, and are united to the soul' as it is called, of the Catholic Church by external communion with her, and by the outward profession of her faith.

To many Catholics, I am sure it must be perplexing to see many Protestants continue to pray the Apostles' Creed, which includes in the body of the prayer, the phrase, "I believe in the Holy Catholic Church" and not consider that perhaps they have a much closer relationship with the Catholic Church than they think. What is not understood by most Catholics, however, is that the term "catholic" or "universal" that was used in the original Apostles' Creed of the second century was first penned by Ignatius of Antioch around A.D. 107, or several hundred years before Roman Emperor Theodosius first defined Roman Catholic Christianity as the official state religion of the Roman Empire.

Despite all of EWTN and Father Di Bruno's efforts to the contrary; if there was any doubt about the Catholic Church's commitment to the Middle Age claim that it was "The One True Church by which one could be saved, that doubt was erased by Pope Benedict XVI, on July 10, 2007, who issued a sixteen-page pronouncement asserting that Jesus established "only one church." According to NBC News Services, Pope Benedict XVI reasserted the universal primacy of the Roman Catholic Church, approving a document that says Orthodox churches were defective and that other Christian denominations were not "true" churches. Additionally, *The Catechism of the Catholic Church (Second Edition)* confirms this teaching on page 215, (para. 816), which reads, "The Second Vatican Council's Decree on Ecumenism explains: 'For it is through Christ's Catholic Church alone, which is the universal help toward salvation, that the fullness of the means of salvation can be obtained.'" Additionally, (CCC para. 846) reads:

> Basing itself on Scripture and Tradition, the Council teaches that the Church, a pilgrim now on earth, is necessary for salvation: the

> one Christ is the mediator and the way of salvation; he is present to us in his body which is the Church. He himself explicitly asserted the necessity of faith and Baptism, and thereby affirmed at the same time the necessity of the Church, which men enter through Baptism as through a door. Hence they could not be saved who, knowing that the Catholic Church was founded as necessary by God through Christ, would refuse either to enter it or to remain in it.

Pope Francis, the First Non-European Pope in Nearly 1,300 years

It remains to be seen if the reform minded Pope Francis, the first non-European pope in nearly 1,300 years, will attempt to change this "Outside the Church (Catholic) there is no salvation" view of the Catholic Church towards non-Catholic Christians. The historical position of the Catholic Church on this subject and the commentary in the new Catechism are baffling and poorly understood by lay Catholics and evangelicals alike; nevertheless they stand as the official position of the Catholic Church and are an impediment to any constructive relationship between Catholics and non-Catholic Christians.

Many Catholics believe that the fact that the Catholic Church has survived for almost two thousand years is a clear sign that she is The One True Church. Even though most Catholics recognize the corruption of the Catholic Church during the Middle Ages, to them surviving in spite of this corruption is further proof of her validity.

World Religions

To trust one's very salvation and eternal destination, however, to the notion that longevity of a particular religious system equals its legitimacy is indeed dangerous. This can be demonstrated by reviewing the longevity of several major world religions:

5,774 years old—Jewish (3760 B.C. is year 1 of the Jewish calendar)
3,714 years old—Hinduism (from 1700 B.C.)
2,614 years old—Buddhism (origins back to 600–100 B.C.)
1,981 years old—Christianity (from 33 A.D.)
1,690 years old—Roman Catholicism (dates from 313 A.D.)
1,387 years old—Islam (Founded by Mohammed around 627 A.D.)
184 years old—Mormonism (founded by Joseph Smith in 1830)

Religions of the world offer only two possibilities: either one can be good enough to be right with God, or one cannot be good enough to be right with God. "*In a word you must be made perfect as your heavenly Father is perfect*" (Matthew

5:48). So, the standard for man is perfection, and God cannot be satisfied by anything less than perfection because He is absolute and perfect holiness. The idea that man can live a good enough life on his own to satisfy God is Satan's greatest deception. The biblical standard is "*All men have sinned and are deprived of the glory of God. All men are now undeservedly justified by the gift of God, through the redemption wrought* of *in Jesus Christ*" (Romans 3:23–24).

World religions are movements of human achievement. They teach that if you are respectable you will go to heaven. The Parable of the Pharisee and the tax collector as told by Christ in Luke 18:9–14 clearly demonstrates the counter-intuitive principle in true Christianity that you cannot be saved by your own goodness. The Pharisee was as decent and religious as any man could be; he fasted as required, gave tithes, prayed, and memorized Scriptures, but the tax collector was justified, not the Pharisee. Jesus said in verse 14, "*Believe Me, this man went home from the temple justified but the other did not. For everyone who exalts himself shall be humbled while he who humbles himself shall be exalted.*" True Christianity is not a religion but rather a personal relationship between God and man.

The 10 Commandments

God gave Moses His law in the Ten Commandments so that man would understand what sin was. Many people feel that because they have not murdered someone, or committed adultery, or robbed a bank that they have kept the Ten Commandments and are worthy of God's grace and redemption. But God says if you have even hated someone you are guilty of murder, and God said that whoever even looks at someone with lust has already committed adultery in his or her heart (see Matthew 5:21–28).

Based on the Ten Commandments, we have to admit our guilt in the eyes of God. It is easy for us to come to this conclusion on our own if we are honest with ourselves. If God were to judge us by the Ten Commandments on judgment day, would we be found innocent or guilty? If we say guilty, does that mean we go to hell or heaven? Some might say heaven, because God is forgiving. This logic, however, would not work in a court of law. If we are found guilty of murder, rape, or robbery, will we be able to convince the judge to let us go by telling him that we know that he is a forgiving man, so we want him to set us free? If he is an honest judge, will he set us free? Certainly, he will not! The judge would be bound by law to do what is right. The same is true of God, as He is bound by His own character to do what is right. God could by no means clear the guilty; that would make God corrupt. Therefore, the very thing that people think will save them on judgment day will actually condemn them.

Repent and Trust in the Savior, Jesus Christ

What God commands us to do in the gospel is to repent. Our response must be to repent and trust in the Savior. We can't earn our way into heaven or pray our way into heaven. God must save us purely out of His mercy. Our response to this message of salvation is to turn our back on sin once and for all, and turn to God with a surrendered heart while embracing the Savior and trusting in Him alone. Don't trust in your own goodness to save you; trust in the only Savior that can save you, Christ Jesus. Once that is done, you can have confidence that you have been born of the Spirit of God. He will give you a new heart, with new desires, power, and strength to walk in His ways.

When you consider God's Commandments and the previously mentioned major religions of the world, and the fact that recent surveys taken in the United States indicate that 77 percent (Gallup 2012) of the population call themselves Christian, it would appear that most people who call themselves Christian likely believe that they are saved and heaven-bound as part of The One True Church. The Bible paints a very different picture. In Matthew 7:14, Jesus tells us, "*But how narrow is the gate that leads to life, how rough the road, and how few there are who find it.*" With this dichotomy, what is the truth?

I Will Build My Church; and the Gates of Hades Will Not Overpower It

The Catholic Catechism states, ". . . Indeed, from the incarnate Word's descent to us, all Christian churches everywhere have held and hold the great Church that is here

[at Rome] to be their only basis and foundation since, according to the Savior's promise, the gates of hell have never prevailed against her." (CCC para. 834)

The Bible and history, however, stand as examples against this claim. In the Book of Revelation, written by John around A.D. 94–96, Christ says that five of the seven churches mentioned in Chapters two and three were in some level of apostasy, teaching error and tolerating corruption. The Church at Thyatira was teaching "the deep things of Satan, and was corrupt," Sardis was called a "dead church," Pergamum was a "compromising church," Laodicea was "lukewarm," and Ephesus had "left their first love"—Christ. Clearly, the gates of hell had prevailed against these churches, which by Catholic definition would be Catholic. Satan is victorious anytime churches are preaching error! Christ promises to take away their "lampstands," the light of life of the gospel, unless churches repent and reform!

The last three popes have now admitted to the horrific sins of the church during the Inquisition, which lasted over six hundred years, the crusades, and to the various scandals and corruption identified in the contemporary Catholic Church, and they have apologized and promised, "Never again." Unfortunately, many Catholic teachings are still in conflict with Scripture and need repentance and reform.

The One True Church

The answer to the question: who is "The One True Church," can be found in the Book of Revelation 3:4, where Christ says, "*. . . you have a few people in Sardis who have not soiled their garments; and they will walk with Me in white because they are worthy*." In Revelation 2:24–25, Christ speaking to those in Thyatira, who were not tolerating the evils of Jezebel; "*But I say to you, 'the rest' who are in Thyatira, who do not hold this teaching, who have not known the deep things of Satan, as I call them—on you I place no further burden. In any case, hold fast to what you have until I come*." Satan had overcome the five local physical churches, but Satan could not overcome the spirits of true individual believers in those five churches.

It is clear from these passages that The One True Church Christ speaks of cannot be an institutional church that Satan can prevail against, as he did with each of these churches, but could only be those spiritual individuals, a remnant in theses churches, who were truly saved, that Satan could never separate from God (see Romans 8:31–39).

We know from the Book of Ephesians that Christ loved the church and gave Himself up for her, "*to make her holy, purifying her in the bath of water by the power of the word, to present to himself a glorious church, holy and immaculate, without a stain or wrinkle or anything of that sort*" (Ephesians 5:26-27). Saving grace makes believers holy by the agency of the Word of God so that they may be a pure bride. It is clear from these verses that this spotless church could only be those individual believers that God elected from the beginning, representing the Body of Christ of all ages, and would by definition exclude the institutional church, which has clearly not been spotless or blameless through the ages.

The truth is that no church or religion can deliver salvation for us. The One True Church is not a denomination but rather all true believers in the Lord Jesus Christ made up of God's redeemed from all the ages—all born of the Holy Spirit—all drawn from a single faith in the Bible. Its members are found everywhere. The One True Church lives when all worldly things are taken from it. It does not need cathedrals, church buildings, or vestments. The One True Church in the New Testament was never a denomination; it was the Body of Christ in all ages. Our salvation is personal and individual, not institutional.

"The church is composed of all who place their faith in Jesus Christ, who are then baptized of the Holy Spirit into one united spiritual body, the church (1 Corinthians 12:12–13), the bride of Christ (2 Corinthians 11:2; Ephesians 5:23–32; Revelation 19:7–8), of which Christ is the Head (Ephesians 1:22; 4:15; Colossians 1:18). The formation of the church, the

Body of Christ, began on the Day of Pentecost (Acts 2:1–21, 38–47) and will be completed at the coming of Christ for His own at the rapture of the church (1 Corinthians 15:51–52; 1 Thessalonians 4:13–18). The church is a unique spiritual organism designed by Christ, made up of all born-again believers in this present age (Ephesians 2:11; 3:6). The church is distinct from Israel (1 Corinthians 10:32), a mystery not revealed until this age (Ephesians 3:1–6; 5:32). The establishment and continuity of local churches is clearly taught and defined in the New Testament Scriptures (Acts 14:23, 27; 20:17, 28; Galatians 1:2; Philippians 1:1; 1 Thessalonians 1:1; 2 Thessalonians 1:1), and that the members of the "One Spiritual Body" are directed to associate themselves together in local assemblies (1 Corinthians 11:18–20; Hebrews 10:25). The one supreme authority for the church Is not the church herself, but rather Jesus Christ, as revealed in the Scriptures (1 Corinthians 11:3; Ephesians 1:22; Colossians 1:8)" (Grace Community Church, Sun Valley, CA).

III

The Bible

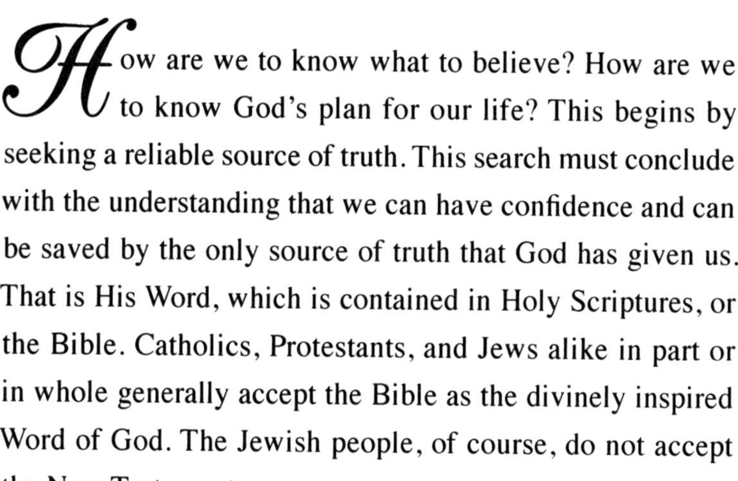

How are we to know what to believe? How are we to know God's plan for our life? This begins by seeking a reliable source of truth. This search must conclude with the understanding that we can have confidence and can be saved by the only source of truth that God has given us. That is His Word, which is contained in Holy Scriptures, or the Bible. Catholics, Protestants, and Jews alike in part or in whole generally accept the Bible as the divinely inspired Word of God. The Jewish people, of course, do not accept the New Testament.

The Catholic Church recognizes the Bible as a sacred book but not as the sole and final authority for truth. All of the teachings, doctrines, and dogmas of the Roman Catholic Church are contained in the Catechism of the Catholic Church (CCC), promulgated by Pope John Paul II, and endorsed by Joseph Cardinal Ratzinger (Pope Benedict XVI), copyright 1994. The CCC is a 900-page volume of 2,865 paragraphs of

Catholic doctrine. The Catholic Church teaches that, "Both Scripture and Tradition must be accepted and honored with equal sentiments of devotion and reverence" (CCC para. 82, 95).

The Catholic Church teaches that the Bible is not the all-sufficient rule of faith, but that revelation found in tradition is also necessary—often based on the following Scripture passage from the Book of John:

> *There are still many other things that Jesus did, yet if they were written about in detail, I doubt there would be room enough in the entire world to hold the books to record them* (John 21:25).

Most Roman Catholic traditions, however, are human traditions that have been developed since the time of the apostles' teachings: The Council of Clermont approved Indulgences in 1096; Purgatory became a dogma in 1439; Mary's Immaculate Conception became a dogma in 1854; Papal Infallibility in 1870; and the Assumption of Mary into heaven was made a dogma of the Church in 1950.

Since none of these are divinely inspired apostolic traditions taught in the first century they should be rejected because they are not found in God's Word, and are often in conflict with the Scriptures. The Word of God in the Bible does not evolve, it is a constant. We are not to add to it or subtract from it. The Book of Revelation reads, *"I myself give witness to all who hear the prophetic words of this book. If anyone adds to these words, God will visit him with all the plagues described herein! If anyone takes from the words of this prophetic book, God will take away his share in the tree of life and the holy city described here"* (Revelation 22:18-19)!

These are not the first warnings against altering God's Word by adding to it or subtracting from it. We read in Deuteronomy, *"In your observance of the commandments of the Lord, which I will enjoin upon you, you shall not add to what I command you or subtract from it"* (Deuteronomy 4:2). The Word that God had given to Israel through Moses was complete and sufficient to direct the people. Anything that adulterated or contradicted God's law would not be tolerated.

We read in Proverbs, *"Every Word of God is tested; he is a shield to those who take refuge in him. Add nothing to his words, least he reprove you, and you be exposed as a deceiver"* (Proverbs 30:5-6). God's Word has been tested and found to be without impurity or error. To add to God's Word with man-made tradition or "revelation" is to deny God as the standard of truth. God is not like man that He changes His mind or adds or subtracts from His inspired truth in the Bible, because he had an afterthought. No, God is perfect in His Word and in every other way.

Note the past tense of the verbs given in the following verses:

I was already fully intent on writing you, beloved, about the salvation we share. But now I feel obliged to write and encourage you to fight hard for the faith delivered (emphasis added) once for all to the saints (Jude 3).

"*Therefore, brothers, stand firm. Hold fast to the traditions you received (emphasis added) from us, either by our word or by letter*" (2 Thessalonians 2:15).

At the time of Jude's epistle (A.D. 68-70) the churches already had twenty-one of the twenty-seven books of the New Testament in written form, and the apostle Paul was likely preaching many of the divine traditions that he would later pen in his epistles. Clearly, Paul did not have in mind a body of extra biblical tradition that is equal to God's revelation in Scripture; in fact, the Bible condemns such human traditions (Isaiah 29:13; Matthew 15:3; Mark7:8-9; Colossians 2:8). The Greek word for tradition literally means, "things handed down" and refers here to divine revelation, whether given by word of mouth or by letter, through Paul and the other apostles. This divine revelation (oral and written) ceased with the death of the last apostle, John, just as the miracles that the apostles performed ceased at their death. The past tense of the verbs in the above passages from Jude and Paul signify that the believers had already received in written or oral form the fullness of the faith of the gospel. No further "revelation," such as human tradition, was needed. God had spoken!

A) Short History of the Bible

The Bible was communicated through godly men writing down what they experienced through the Holy Spirit from the very beginning. We know from Jude 1:14 that Enoch, for example, was recording events even in his day, and he was seventh in line from Adam. The first book of the Bible is Genesis, which in Greek means "origins." The Hebrew title for the first book of Moses (Old Testament) is derived from the very first word, translated, "in the beginning." The theme of the Bible from start (Genesis) to finish (Revelation) is the redemption of mankind.

Creationist scholar, Professor Andy McIntosh of Leeds University in England, writes, "Many think the phrase, 'this is the history of . . .' or 'this is the book of generations of . . .' (Genesis 5:1 is an example) is referring to written documents." Dr. McIntosh goes on to say, "Old written languages like Chinese have a memory of events in Eden, and so the biblical record was in written form very early on. Moses compiled the first five books, almost certainly from existing (at the time) written records."

For many centuries, the Bible existed only in handwritten manuscript form. One of the many means of determining the accuracy of the Bible today is the number of copies of the manuscripts available from past history. There are more than 24,000 manuscript copies of portions of the New Testament in existence today, some from as early as 50–60 A.D. This provides scholars with a wealth of documentation to be able to delineate quite closely what the original manuscripts contained. There is some suggestion that actual portions of the original gospel is likely contained in some of the manuscripts in hand today. In comparison to the vast array of copies of portions of Bible manuscripts available to us today, only seven copies of the work of historian Pliny (61–113 A.D.) and only five copies of philosopher Aristotle's (384–322 B.C.) works have survived until today, according to McDowell's *Evidence That Demands a Verdict*.

It is clear that the manuscript copies that are in our possession today were written and compiled quite early, and a number of them are several hundred years before the earliest copy of a secular manuscript. This clearly shows the importance that early Christians placed on preserving the accuracy of the Scriptures.

All books of the Bible were completed by about A. D. 100, and it is clear that Jews wrote all but just a few of these sixty-six books. The Bible has one Divine Author, although it was written by nearly forty human writers.

The Old Testament deals largely with the history and religious life of ancient Israel from about 3700 B.C. to around 400 B.C. (Genesis was written about 1400 B.C.). John the Baptist was the last of the Old Testament Prophets and the first New Testament Prophet and brought the new law era—the era of fulfillment of the Old Testament. The New Testament (the Gospel) spans approximately one hundred years. It begins by describing the birth of Jesus Christ and ends about A.D.100. Theologians date the writing of the Book of Revelation about A.D. 94–96. The Old Testament was available in Hebrew, Aramaic, and Greek by the mid-200s B.C. The New Testament was written originally in Greek, and the entire Bible had been translated into Syriac and Latin by the A.D. 100s.

The Catholic Church had Saint Jerome translate the Bible into Latin about A.D. 382. Jerome used the Hebrew Bible as well as Latin and Greek translations of both Testaments. He finally completed the project in A.D. 405. Jerome's version became known as *The Vulgate (translation)* and was the only version of the Bible authorized by the Roman Catholic Church for centuries. The first complete English translation of the Bible appeared in the 1380s and was translated by English theologian and scholar John Wycliffe and his followers. This was handwritten and translated from the Latin Vulgate.

The only significant variation in the Bible used by different religions involves the books of The Apocrypha. The Apocrypha consists of fifteen books or parts of books representing approximately 12 percent of the entire Bible. This includes Tobit, Judith, Wisdom, Sirach, Baruch, Letter of Jeremiah, Prayer of Manasseh, additions to Esther, and 1 and 2 Maccabees. The Apocrypha was received into the Canon of the Catholic Church in 1546 at the Council of Trent. The Hebrew Bible excludes all of the books of The Apocrypha. Most Protestant Bibles omit The Apocrypha entirely, while the Roman Catholic Church incorporates most of the books of The Apocrypha throughout the Old Testament. The word "apocrypha" was defined by the Reformers as, "of questionable authenticity."

The Catholic Church takes credit for establishing the canon of the Bible, but 70 percent of the Bible is the Old Testament, and Jewish rabbis established the canon of the Old Testament by 100 B.C. Historian Philip Schaff writes:

> The Jewish canon, or the Hebrew Bible, was universally received while the apocrypha added to the Greek version of the Septuagint were only in a general way accounted as books suitable for church reading . . . for those books, while they have great historical value, and filled the gap between the Old Testament and the New, all originated after the cessation of prophecy, and they cannot therefore be regarded as inspired, nor are they ever cited by Christ or the apostles (Philip Schaff, *History of the Christian Church*, Book 3, Chapter 9).

> Ultimately, it was God who decided what books belonged in the biblical canon. A book of Scripture belonged in the canon from the moment that God inspired its writing. It was simply a matter of God's convincing His human followers which books should be included in the Bible. No early church council decided on the canon. It was God and God alone who determined which books belonged in the Bible. It was simply a matter of God imparting to His followers what He had already decided. The human process of collecting the books of the Bible was flawed, but God in His sovereignty, and despite our ignorance and stubbornness, brought the early church to the recognition of the books He had inspired (*The Canon of Scripture*, by F. F. Bruce).

There are a number of reasons that the Apocrypha is not considered inspired:

(1) Not one of the Apocrypha books was written in the Hebrew language, which was alone used by the inspired historians and poets of the Old Testament; (2) Not one of the writers lays claim to inspiration; (3) These books were never acknowledged as sacred Scripture by the Jewish church, and therefore were never sanctioned by our Lord; (4) They

were not allowed a place among the sacred books, during the first four centuries of the Christian Church; (5) The Roman Catholic Church herself did not officially canonize the Apocrypha until the Council of Trent (1546 A.D.). This was in part because the Apocrypha contained material that seemed to support certain Catholic doctrines, such as purgatory and praying for the dead; and (6) It was believed by many that the Apocrypha books taught immoral practices, such as lying, suicide, assassination, and magical incantation.

There is a common misconception by some Catholics that the Protestant translations of the Bible are largely different than its Catholic counterparts. With the exception of the Apocrypha, this is not the case as the Bible has virtually the same meaning in all approved translations, even though certain words may vary. For example, in John 10:7 the original Greek is translated into "door" in the Ryrie New American Standard Bible, while the same word is translated "sheep gate" in the New American Catholic Bible.

Differences in the words and phrases used in various Bible translations can be explained by several factors. Jerome translated *The Vulgate* using manuscripts available at that time (OT-Hebrew and Aramaic, NT-Greek) along with earlier Latin translations. This required adaptation of words that did not translate precisely from one language to another. Portions of Holy Scripture in English appeared early in the seventh century, and the first complete English translation was written in 1382, having been translated from the Latin.

In 1525, William Tyndale published the first English translation of the New Testament directly from the original Greek manuscripts. The original English Bibles were in Old English vernacular, which became increasingly difficult to understand as the English language evolved, and translators updated the text with more contemporary language. With all the nuances of the different languages, we find the use of many words and phrases with similar meanings, which vary depending on the particular Bible translation being used. Additionally, translators exhibited human bias when choosing their vocabulary. The important point, however, is that all of the major translations, whether Catholic or Protestant, have a high degree of harmony and convey a consistent message of God's Word.

B) Accuracy of the Bible

The Word, the Bible, the Scriptures cannot be in error, or God's power is limited. The Bible is true and authoritative as evidenced by:

The Unity of the Bible never contradicts itself.

Alleged biblical contradictions turn out to be nothing more than false reasoning on the part of Bible critics. In *How Do We Know The Bible Is True,* author Jason Lisle fleshes out classic claims of biblical contradictions using the "Law of Non-contradiction." The Law of Non-contradiction states that a contradiction cannot be true. Lisle says, "It is impossible to have **A** and not **A** at the same time and in the same relationship."

For example, one of the classic allegations of a Bible contradiction is on the subject of justification, where Romans is claimed to contradict James. Lisle writes "Romans 4:2–3 teaches that Abraham was justified by faith alone, not by works. However, James 2:21, 24 teaches that Abraham was justified by works and not by faith alone. Do we have a contradiction here? We do have **A** and not **A** at the same time, but the relationship differs. Romans 4 is teaching about justification before God; by faith alone Abraham was considered righteous before God. But James 2 is teaching about justification before men (James 2:18); by works (as a result of faith) Abraham was considered righteous before men. There is no contradiction here."

The Bible was scientifically accurate in a primitive world.

All stars look alike to the naked eye. Even when seen through a telescope, they seem to be just points of light. However, analysis of their light spectra, available today, reveals that each is unique and different from all others.

(1 Corinthians 15:41)—Written A.D. 55
"*The sun has a splendor of its own, so has the moon, and the stars have theirs. Even among the stars, one differs from another in brightness.*"

The fact that air has weight was only proven scientifically about 300 years ago. The relative weights of air and water are needed for the efficient functioning of the world's hydrologic cycle, which in turn sustains life on earth.

(Job 28:25)—Written about 2000 B.C
"*He has weighed out the wind, And fixed the scope of the waters.*"

Hydrothermal vents are described in two books of the Bible written before 1400 B.C.—more than 3,000 years before their discovery by science.

(Genesis 7:11)—Written 1445–1405 B.C.
"*In the six hundredth year of Noah's life, in the second month, the seventeenth day of the month, on that day all the fountains of the great abyss burst forth, and the floodgates of the sky were opened.*" Also see Job 38:16.

The witness of many authenticated miracles.

Miracles were performed before witnesses in both the Old Testament and the New Testament, pointing to God and demonstrating His power.

In the Old Testament very credible witnesses such as Abraham, Moses, and Daniel witnessed many miracles.

In the New Testament Jesus fed 5,000 people, starting with just five loaves and two fish (Matthew 14:13–21). Not only was everyone fed, but also there were twelve full baskets of leftovers. The Book of Matthew was written in 50–60 A.D., so many of the 5,000 would still be alive to confirm this event, after the gospels were written.

Even members of the Jewish Sanhedrin Council, who hated Christ and the gospel message, admitted that Peter and John had performed a significant miracle of healing a man who had been lame from birth. In Acts 4:16, we read an account of their discussions: "*What shall we do with these men? Everyone who lives in Jerusalem knows what a remarkable show of power took place through them. We cannot deny it.*"

Jesus healed the blind, cured lepers, healed the deaf, cast out demons, and raised people from the dead during His earthly ministry. Many authenticated these miracles by witnesses, including the apostles and unbelievers.

Jewish historian Flavius Josephus (37-100 A.D.), wrote about many of the amazing works done by Christ and the apostles, but he was not himself a believer.

We know beyond doubt that Christ rose bodily because all four Gospels describe this event. The apostles and hundreds of eyewitnesses all faithfully proclaimed the truth of the miracle of the resurrection. Never was their testimony seriously challenged by contradictory witnesses, nor have they ever been refuted. History vindicates this miracle, and the church affirms it.

History and tradition tells us that most of the apostles died as martyrs, and two were actually crucified, but none recanted their belief in Jesus Christ and His Gospel. It is hard to believe that any man would be willing to die to perpetuate a forgery or a lie.

Hundreds of prophecies were fulfilled to the letter.

Approximately 2,500 prophecies appear in the Bible. About 2,000 of these have already been fulfilled exactly as predicted. The remaining 500 prophecies relate to future times.

For example, some time before 500 B.C. the prophet Daniel proclaimed that Israel's long-awaited Messiah would begin his public ministry 483 years after the issuing of a decree to restore and rebuild Jerusalem (Daniel 9:25–26). He further predicted that Messiah would be "cut-off," or killed, and that this event would take place prior to a second destruction of

Jerusalem. Historical evidence shows that these prophecies were perfectly fulfilled in the life and death on a cross of Jesus Christ.

Archaeological discoveries confirm the Bible's authenticity.

The walls of Jericho did indeed come down, as confirmed by archaeological discovery during the excavation of Jericho. This excavation revealed that the walls of this city did fall just as described in the Book of Joshua in the Bible.

Genesis 14:2 describes five cities of the plain that were once thought by secular scholars to be mythical cities. Ancient documents have now been found that show these cities as part of ancient trade routes.

The historical accuracy of the Bible is undeniable.

Many discoveries over the centuries have established the accuracy of events described in the Bible that has brought increased recognition to the value of the Bible as a source of history.

The Hittites, for example, are mentioned over forty-five times in the Bible (see Joshua 3:10), but no mention of the Hittite Nations are written in secular history. Many, before the twentieth century, considered the Hittites as a fictitious empire. Today you can graduate from the University of Pennsylvania with a doctorate degree in Hittitology.

C) The Bible as the Word of God

While the Bible was not written primarily as a book on science, it was written for a mind of faith, but everywhere it touches on science, history, law, and other disciplines, it is accurate. Nevertheless, the truth of the Bible is obvious to anyone willing to fairly investigate it. The Bible is uniquely consistent and authentic. The previous six points provide evidence that it stands up well to the scrutiny of history, anthropology, archeology, prophecy, and science. The Bible claims to be the Word of God, and it demonstrates this claim by making knowledge possible. It is the standard of standards. Simon Greenleaf, one of history's greatest minds former Harvard law professor, and author of a book on legal evidence, carefully applied the rules of legal evidence to the Gospel accounts in his book, *The Testimony of the Evangelists,* and confidently concluded that the Bible is truth.

Most people in the world know about God, but to truly know who God is on a personal level we must study His Word in the Bible. There are over two thousand references in the Old Testament alone that asserts that God spoke what is written within its pages. The phrase "Word of God" appears over forty times in the New Testament. There are occasions in the Bible when God Himself actually writes Scripture, such as the giving of the Ten Commandments (Exodus 24:12), and the judgment at Belshazzar's feast in Daniel 5. The Bible has endured the attacks of nonbelievers for centuries, without proven contradiction to the findings of history and science. It is also apparent from Scripture itself that God inspired the Bible and intended for Man to search and study Scripture because of the "truths" held there:

2 Peter 1:20–21: "*First you must understand this: there is no prophecy contained in Scripture which is a personal interpretation. Prophecy has never been put forward by man's willing it. It is rather that men impelled by the Holy Spirit have spoke under God's influence.*"

2 Timothy 3:15–17: "*Likewise from your infancy you have known the sacred Scriptures, the source of the wisdom which through faith in Jesus Christ leads to salvation. All Scripture is inspired of God and is useful for teaching—for reproof, correction, and training in holiness so that the man of God may be fully competent and equipped for every good work.*"

1 Peter 1:24: "*. . . but the 'Word of the Lord' endures forever.*"

John 5:39: "*Search the Scriptures in which you think you have eternal life—they also testify on My behalf.*"

1 Thessalonians 5:20–21: "*Do not despise prophecies. Test everything; retain what is good.*"

Matthew 21:42: "*Did you never read in the Scriptures. . . .*"

Proverbs 30:6: "*Add nothing to His Words, least He reprove you, and you be exposed as a deceiver.*"

Galatians 1:9: "*If anyone preaches a Gospel to you other than the one you received, let a curse be upon him!*"

Revelation 22:18,19: "*If anyone adds to these words, God will visit him with all the plagues described herein!*"

Matthew 22:29: "*Jesus replied: 'You are badly misled because you fail to understand the Scriptures and the power of God.'*"

Matthew 4:4: "*Scripture has it: 'Not on bread alone is man to live but on every utterance that comes from the mouth of God.'*"

IV

Characteristics of the APOLSTOLIC CHURCH

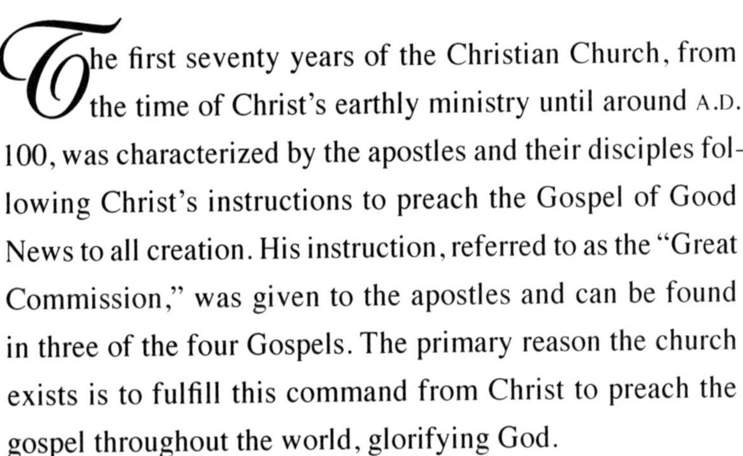

The first seventy years of the Christian Church, from the time of Christ's earthly ministry until around A.D. 100, was characterized by the apostles and their disciples following Christ's instructions to preach the Gospel of Good News to all creation. His instruction, referred to as the "Great Commission," was given to the apostles and can be found in three of the four Gospels. The primary reason the church exists is to fulfill this command from Christ to preach the gospel throughout the world, glorifying God.

Matthew 28:18–20: "*Jesus came forward and addressed them in these words: 'Full authority has been given to Me both in heaven and on earth; go therefore, and make disciples of all nations. Baptize them in the name of the Father, and of the Son, and of the Holy Spirit.' Teach them to carry out everything I have commanded you. And know that I am with you always, until the end of the world!*" (Faith first, baptism second.)

Luke 24:45–47: "*Then He opened their minds to the understanding of the Scriptures. He said to them: 'Thus it is written that the Messiah must suffer and rise from the dead on the third day. In His name, penance (repentance) for the remission of sins is to be preached to all nations, beginning in Jerusalem.*" (Salvation through faith in His name.)

Mark 16:15–16: "*Then He told them: 'Go into the whole world and proclaim the Good News to all creation. The man who believes in it and accepts baptism will be saved; the man who refuses to believe in it will be condemned.*'" (Faith first, baptism second.)

The Book of Acts, written by the apostle Luke, is the first work of church history ever penned. Acts records the initial response to the Great Commission. It provides information on the first three decades of the church's existence, with information found nowhere else in the New Testament. Acts is primarily a historical narrative, as opposed to the theological approach of Romans or Hebrews, for example.

The First Thirty Years of Christian Church History

Acts begins with the coming of the Holy Spirit on the day of Pentecost and ends with Paul's arrival and imprisonment in Rome, where he was able to preach the gospel in the world's capital. The thirty years of church history covered by acts were important years of transition. The gospel was first preached to the Jews, and the early church was composed largely of Jewish believers. As more and more Gentiles were converted, the Church became distinct from Judaism. In his introduction to the Book of Acts, in *The MacArthur New Testament Commentary,* John MacArthur writes, "With the epistles, but without Acts, we would have much difficulty understanding the flow of the early history of the church. With it we have a core history around which to assemble the data in the epistles, enriching our comprehension of them. The book follows the ministry of Peter, then of Paul. From it we learn principles for discipling believers, building the church, and evangelizing the world."

The first twelve chapters of Acts feature the preaching and works of Peter, Stephen, Philip, Barnabas, and James. From chapter 13 to the end, the dominant person is the apostle Paul. Chapter one begins after the resurrection when Christ said to the apostles, "*You will receive power when the Holy Spirit comes down on you; then you are to be My witnesses both in Jerusalem, and in all of Judea and Samaria, yes, even to the ends of the earth*" (Acts 1:8). Matthias was chosen to replace

Judas, who had betrayed Jesus, fulfilling the Old Testament prophecy in Psalms, "*Let his homestead be made desolate, and let no one dwell in it; and, let another man take his office*," and so the apostles were restored to the original twelve before they began to fulfill The Great Commission.

The Holy Spirit came on the apostles, their disciples, and all believers at Pentecost as the Church was founded. Peter preached to the crowd gathered, "*You must reform (repent) and be baptized, each one of you, in the name of Jesus Christ, that your sins may be forgiven; and you will receive the gift of the Holy Spirit*" (Acts 2:38). On that day, those that were saved by receiving the Word of Jesus Christ, and were baptized numbered around three thousand souls.

The Church continued to grow as the apostles preached the gospel of repentance, healed people, and endured persecution. One day Peter and John were going up to the temple at the ninth hour to pray and preach. They came across a man asking for alms, who had been lame from birth. Peter ordered the man to walk, in the name of Jesus Christ the Nazarene, and the man leaped up and began to walk, and all the people saw him walking and praising God. Peter and John praised the God of Abraham, Isaac, and Jacob, the God of their fathers who glorified Jesus, who had healed the lame man. As they were preaching the Good News in Solomon's Portico, many believed, and the number of men who were saved that day numbered some five thousand.

Peter and John were arrested by the priests and the Sadducees, put in jail overnight, and forbidden to preach the name of Jesus. They appeared before the Sanhedrin Council the next day, but they could not deny the incredible miracle that had been performed on the lame man. They commanded the apostles not to preach or teach the name of Jesus, but they refused to comply, so the Sanhedrin threatened them, but let them go.

The power of the Church continued to grow. At the hands of the apostles many signs and wonders were taking place among the people; and they were all with one accord in Solomon's portico. "*Nevertheless more and more believers, men and women in great numbers, were continually added to the Lord. The people carried the sick out into the streets and laid them on cots and pallets, so that when Peter came by at least his shadow might fall on any one of them*" (Acts 5:14–15). They were arrested again, flogged, but let go, but they kept on teaching and preaching Jesus as the Christ, and in the temple.

Stephen Becomes the First Christian Martyr

Through the powerful preaching of Stephen and the signs and wonders that he was performing, the Word continued to spread, and the number of disciples, including many priests, increased greatly in Jerusalem. Stephen was accused of blasphemy and brought before the Council with false witnesses, but Stephen was able to give his testimony. In closing his preaching he told the Council, "*Was there ever any prophet whom your fathers did not persecute? In their day, they put to death those who foretold the coming of the Just One; now you in your turn have become His betrayers and murderers. You who received the law through the ministry of angels have not observed it*" (Acts 7:52–53). When the Council heard this, they became angry, drove Stephen out of the city, and stoned him to death. The crowd stoning Stephen laid aside their robes at the feet of a young man named Saul from Tarsus.

Christ is preached in Samaria by Philip, and many are amazed at Philip's preaching of the Word and the signs that he was performing. Unclean spirits were cast out of many, and many who had been paralyzed and lame were healed. "*But once they began to believe in the good news that Philip preached about the kingdom of God and the name of Jesus Christ, men and women alike accepted baptism*" (Acts 8:12). Even a sorcerer named Simon believed, and after being baptized continued on with Philip, and he was constantly amazed at the signs and miracles constantly taking place.

The Apostle Paul's Conversion on the Road to Damascus

Saul (Paul) is converted on the Damascus Road, is filled with the Holy Spirit, is baptized, and he immediately began preaching Christ in the synagogues saying, "*He is the Son of God*." Many were still frightened of Saul's reputation for persecuting the believers, but Barnabas befriended Saul and brought him to the apostles and told them about his conversion and bold preaching of the name of the Lord. At this time the church was peacefully prospering in Judea, Samaria, and Galilee and continued to grow in number.

While in Joppa Peter restores life to a disciple named Dorcus. While in Joppa, He is invited by a centurion convert named Cornelius to come to Caesarea to speak to his entire household, which included both Jews and Gentiles. While preaching to Cornelius' household, the Holy Spirit descended upon all those who were listening to the message. The Jews were amazed, because the gift of the Holy Spirit was poured out on the Gentiles also. Peter ordered them baptized, both Jew and Gentile alike.

Paul's First Missionary Journey

Barnabas met Saul in Tarsus and brought him to Antioch, where they spent a year together, teaching many who became disciples. The disciples were first called Christians at Antioch. Barnabas and Saul, soon to be renamed Paul, along with John, who was also called Mark, began what would later be called Paul's first missionary journey in 46 A.D., which would take two years to complete.

They preached in the synagogues and baptized those that believed the gospel of Jesus Christ in Salamis and Paphos on Cyprus, in Perga in Pamphylia, in Antioch in Pisidia, in Iconium, in Lycaonia, and Lystra and Derbe. After they preached the gospel in Derbe, they returned to Lystra and to Iconium, and Antioch in Pisidia, back to Perga, strengthening the souls of the many disciples converted, encouraging them to continue in the faith. They appointed elders in the local churches and having prayed with fasting, they commended them to the Lord in whom they had believed. They continued their journey to Attalia, and from there they sailed back to Antioch in Syria in 48 A.D., where they reported to the church all the things that God had done with them and how He had opened the door of faith to the Gentiles. Many were converted on Paul's first missionary journey, but Paul and Barnabas paid a great price as they were persecuted and stoned by the jealous Jews along the way.

Paul's Second Missionary Journey

Paul's second missionary journey began in 49 A.D., and included Silas, who Paul took in place of John Mark, who had deserted him in Pamphylia on his first missionary journey. They went up from Jerusalem to Syria and Cilicia, strengthening the churches. Paul and Silas went on to Derbe and Lystra, where Timothy joined them. The churches were increasing in number daily. They went on to Troas, and from there God called them to Macedonia. They arrived in Philippi, which was a leading city of the district of Macedonia, a

Roman colony. While in Philippi a woman named Lydia was listening to Paul preach, and the Lord opened her heart to respond to the things spoken by Paul. Then she and her household were baptized.

Paul and Silas were imprisoned because they commanded an evil spirit come out of a slave girl whose master was profiting from her activity. While in prison an earthquake occurred, jarring the prison doors open, and the jailer started to take his life for fear that his prisoners had escaped. Paul stopped the jailer from harming himself, and the jailer asked what must I do to be saved? They said, "*Believe in the Lord Jesus, and you will be saved; you and your household*" (Acts 16:31). They spoke the gospel to all who were in his household, who believed, and immediately they were all baptized.

They came to Thessalonica, having traveled through Amphipolis and Apollonia. As was Paul's custom he went to the synagogue and preached Christ as Lord for three consecutive Sabbaths. Some of the Jews were persuaded and joined Paul and Silas, along with a large number of the God-fearing Greeks and a number of the leading women. The Jews became jealous and formed a mob to attack Paul and Silas, but the brethren immediately sent Paul and Silas by night to Berea, and when they arrived, they went directly into the synagogue of the Jews to preach.

In Berea, "*Each day they studied the Scriptures to see whether these things were so. Many of them came to believe, as did numerous influential Greek women and men*"

(Acts17:11–12). When the Jews in Thessalonica found out that the Word of God had been proclaimed by Paul in Berea, they came there stirring up the crowds. The brethren immediately sent Paul out with escorts to Athens. Timothy and Silas stayed behind in Berea.

Paul Preaches in the Areopagus in Athens

In Athens Paul stood to preach in the Areopagus saying, "*Men of Athens, I observe that in every respect you are scrupulously religious*" (Acts 17:22). He preached the gospel of repentance trying to explain to them that the God who made the world did not dwell in temples made with hands, as though He needed something from man. When he spoke of the resurrection of the dead, the crowd sneered, as Greeks did not believe in bodily resurrection. They agreed, however, to listen to him again. But some men joined him and believed, including Dionysius the Areopagite and a woman named Damaris along with a number of others.

After Athens Paul went to Corinth, where he was teaching and reasoning in the synagogue every Sabbath in an effort to persuade both Jews and Greeks. When Silas and Timothy joined him from Macedonia, Paul began devoting himself completely to the Word, testifying to the Jews that Jesus was the Christ. When they resisted and blasphemed, Paul shook his garments and said to them, "*Your blood be on your own heads! I am clean. From now on I will go to the Gentiles*"

(Acts 18:6). Crispus, the leader of the synagogue, believed in the Lord, and many Corinthians believed and were baptized after they heard the Word.

After many days in Corinth, Paul put out to sea for Syria. He arrived in Ephesus and went to the synagogue to reason with the Jews. They asked him to stay longer, but he set sail for Caesarea, and then went up (description of geography) to greet the church in Jerusalem, ending his second missionary journey, likely in the summer of 52 A.D.

Paul returned to Ephesus where he continued to speak boldly for three months in the synagogue about the kingdom of God. Those believers, who had been baptized into John's baptism, were re-baptized in the name of the Lord Jesus. God was performing many miracles by the hands of Paul, so that handkerchiefs were even carried from his body to the sick, and the diseases left them, and the evil spirits went out.

Paul's Third Missionary Journey

Paul's third missionary journey, and his longest, from 54–58 A.D. started from Antioch in Syria to Macedonia. He traveled through Tarsus, Derbe, Lystra, Iconium, Antioch in Pisidia, Ephesus, Troas, Philippi, Apollona, and on to Athens. As he passed through many districts on his way to Greece, he counseled and challenged the believers in their faith. Paul stayed in Greece for three months until a plot was formed against him by the Jews as he was about to set sail for

Syria. He decided to return to Syria through Macedonia. He traveled through Corinth, Berea, Thessalonica, Amphipolis, and Philippi, exhorting the faithful, on the way to Troas where Sopater of Berea, Aristarchus and Secundus of the Thessalonians, Gaius of Derbe, and Timothy and others waited for him.

Paul and his traveling companions gathered with the church for worship on their first Sunday in Troas, and Paul preached his message until midnight. A young man sitting on a window sill fell asleep and fell to his death. Paul miraculously restored him to life, and the worshipers went back up to the upper room where they broke bread (took communion), and they stayed until daybreak listening to Paul.

The companions and Paul traveled from Troas, past Ephesus, to Miletus, where Paul asked the elders of the church at Ephesus to come to him so he could encourage and instruct them. Paul sensed that he would never see them again, and he wanted to warn them against false teachers who would come after him. Paul prayed with them, embraced them, and set sail for Jerusalem, traveling through Rhodes, Patara, Tyre, Ptolemais, and Caesarea. Arriving in Jerusalem, completing his journey, Paul met with James and the brethren, and related all the things that God had done among the Gentiles through his ministry. When they heard this, they began glorifying God.

After the completion of the days of purification, Paul entered the temple and was arrested by the Jews and accused of preaching against the Jews and the Law to men everywhere.

Roman soldiers came to save him from the mob, which was trying to kill him. Paul was allowed to address the mob and gave a full account of his life as a Jewish zealot, his conversion on the Damascus Road, and the way to salvation through Jesus the Christ. The mob asked for his death, but Paul told the soldiers that he was a Roman citizen, which led to his release, and Paul was allowed to appear before the Sanhedrin, where he again was able to tell his story, which caused some dissension between the Pharisees and Sadducees present. Unhappy with Paul's words, forty zealous Jews band together to kill Paul, but the Romans found out and sent Paul under armed guard to Caesarea to appear before Governor Felix.

Paul's Fourth Missionary Journey

Paul was a Roman prisoner of Felix and Porcius Festus for two years but finally asked to be tried by Caesar in Rome. In the Autumn of 60 A.D. Paul, along with other prisoners, boarded a ship for Rome. This travel to Rome considered Paul's fourth missionary journey. Paul traveled through Caesarea, Sidon, Crete, was shipwrecked on Malta, traveled to Syracuse, and Rhegium in route, preaching along the way. In Rome Paul was allowed to live by himself guarded only by a soldier. He was able to receive visitors and continued to preach the Gospel. Paul stayed two full years in Rome in his own rented quarters and welcomed all who came to him, preaching the kingdom of God and teaching concerning the Lord Jesus Christ with all openness, unhindered.

An End and a Beginning

The final chapters of Acts are both an end and a beginning. Luke, Paul's friend and traveling companion, brought the early history of the church to a close. The text covers the expansion of the church geographically, from its birth in Jerusalem on the Day of Pentecost, to Judea, Samaria, and most of the Roman Empire, consisting of all the provinces bordering upon the Mediterranean Sea, and also some lands outside its boundaries, especially upon the east. Its membership was increasingly Gentile and decreasingly Jewish, for as the gospel gained a following in the pagan world, the Jews drew away from it, but the leadership of the church was heavily Jewish, with the apostle Luke the only Gentile to pen any books of Scripture.

Every local church congregation was an independent unit. There was no super hierarchy of any kind tying these congregations together or exercising authority over them. There were only two kinds of officers in the congregation—the elders and deacons. The elders were the superior officers, and all of these elders were equal to each other. They were sometimes called pastors or bishops, and they were always married men, with believing children.

Catholic Traditions Unknown in First Seventy Years of Christianity

Through the tireless efforts of the apostle Paul, local churches were founded, strengthened, given leaders, and protected from false teachers. The first thirty years of the church, while most of the apostles were still alive, was the purest presentation that the gospel would experience, because the leaders (the apostles) had been handpicked and trained by Christ Himself, and they carried out His instructions called, "the Great Commission," with the power and perfection of the Holy Spirit.

It is instructive to note that in the Book of Acts during the first thirty years of church history preaching and teaching the gospel is mentioned forty times, baptizing is mentioned twenty-seven times, and breaking bread (communion) is mentioned only five times. It is clear that the most important elements of church ministry were preaching the Word and baptizing those that believed, and then breaking bread to remember Christ's death on the cross. Communion (Lord's Supper, Eucharist), while important, was clearly not the central theme of Christianity. We know from Acts and later books in the Bible that in the first seventy years of Christianity, when the apostles and their disciples were alive and preaching, there was no mass, no transubstantiation, no Christian priesthood, no pope or papal infallibility, no infant baptism, no indulgences, no confession to a priest for absolution, no purgatory, no statues or relics, and no prayers to Mary or the saints.

V

Traditions AND history of the Roman Catholic Church

After the time of the apostles and their disciples, when Constantine was emperor of the Roman Empire, the Catholic Church began to evolve into a structured religious system. By A.D. 500, the Catholic Church now reflected a number of the laws, traditions, and rituals of ancient Israel. Like Israel prior to A.D.70, the Catholic Church now had a priesthood. There were priestly vestments similar to those described in the Old Testament for the Jewish priesthood. A sacrificial system was established with the sacrifice of the Mass at its center. Like the Jewish Temple, an altar was now present in Catholic Churches. Just as the Jewish faith has seven holidays where special services are held at the synagogue, the Catholic Church today has six Holy Days of Obligation, where mass attendance is mandatory. In Catholic Churches, there is a tabernacle near the altar to house the consecrated host (Blessed Sacrament), which is believed to be the actual body of Christ, while the Ark of the Covenant was placed in the tabernacle in the Holy of Holies in the Jewish Temple to provide a place where God might dwell among His people. In many ways, the Roman Catholic Church began to evolve into a religious system that today looks a lot like the ancient Jewish religion. Consider the following:

	Jewish Religion Before A.D. 70	Apostolic Christianity A.D. 33–100	Roman Catholicism After A.D. 500
A Sacrificial System	YES	NO	YES
A Priesthood	YES	NO	YES
Priestly Vestments (different from worshipers)	YES	NO	YES
An Altar as part of Temple or Church Service	YES	NO	YES
A Tabernacle to house an object of worship	YES	NO	YES
Dietary Laws-Kosher, No meat on Friday, prescribed days of Fasting.	YES	NO	YES
Many Traditions and Rituals	YES	NO	YES
Special Holidays requiring mandatory Attendance at Temple or Church—7 Temple Holidays—6 Holy Days of Obligation in U.S.	YES	NO	YES

Earliest Christians were almost exclusively Jewish. This is confirmed by the Epistle of James, which is accepted by theologians as the earliest book of the New Testament written around A.D. 44–49, or less than fifteen years after Christ's crucifixion. James refers to his audience as "brethren" fifteen times, which was a common term among first century Jews. *James* is Jewish in its content and has more than forty references to the Old Testament. After Constantine, when

Christianity became the state religion in the Holy Roman Empire, Jewish religious traditions slipped into the Roman Catholic Church as apostolic theology and discipline were sacrificed for mass conversions to Roman Catholicism.

In the book of Galatians, Paul tells the Churches of Galatia to refrain from going back to the laws, traditions, and rituals that they practiced before becoming followers of Christ. Paul tells the Galatians in Galatians 3:1–9:

> *You senseless Galatians! Who has cast a spell over you–you before whose eyes Jesus Christ was displayed to view upon His cross? I want to learn only one thing from you: How did you receive the Spirit? Was it through observance of the law or through faith in what you heard? How could you be so stupid? After beginning in the Spirit, are you now to end in the flesh?. . . Is it because you observe the law or because you have faith in what you heard that God lavishes the Spirit on you and works wonders in your midst? Consider the case of Abraham: He 'believed God, and it was credited to him justice.' This means that those who believe are sons of Abraham. Because Scripture saw in advance that God's way of justifying the Gentiles would be through faith, it foretold*

this good news to Abraham: 'All nations shall be blessed in you.' Thus it is that all who believe are blessed along with Abraham, the man of faith.

Paul was reinforcing that as Christians, the Galatians were justified and made right with God through their faith, not due to observance of Jewish law, ritual, traditions, or good works.

Justification Is by Faith Alone, by Christ Alone, for the Glory of God Alone

How then does God justify man without lowering His perfect standard? One of the best summaries in Scriptures of this work of justification can be found in Paul's Second Epistle to the Corinthians. Paul says, "*For our sakes God made Him who did not know sin, to be sin, so that in Him we might become the very holiness of God*" (2 Corinthians 5:21). "Holiness" in most texts is translated from the Greek as "righteousness."

Dr. John MacArthur, author, pastor, and theologian, summarizes the meaning of this verse in the following manner: "On the cross God treated Christ as if He had committed all of the sins of every sinner who would ever believe, so that He could treat believers as if they had lived Christ's perfect life."

Paul is saying to the Corinthians, and by extension to today's Christians, that they are justified by faith alone, by Christ on the cross alone, for the glory of God alone. Therefore, faith is not by our doing, but by God's grace, which naturally produces good works, but good works cannot produce saving faith! Good works are a natural and intended result of one's salvation through faith in Jesus Christ, but good works themselves can never lead to salvation. With this information, what can be said about key Catholic doctrines that appear to be man-made traditions rather than the beliefs and teachings of the apostles?

Mass–The Catechism of the Catholic Church describes the sacrifice of the Mass in the following words: "The liturgy of the Eucharist unfolds according to a fundamental structure which has been preserved throughout the centuries down to our own day. It displays two great parts that form a fundamental unity:

- the gathering, the liturgy of the Word, with readings, homily, and general intercessions;
- the liturgy of the Eucharist, with presentation of the bread and wine, the consecratory thanksgiving, and communion. The liturgy of the Word and liturgy of the Eucharist together form 'one single act of worship;' the Eucharist table is set for us is the table both of the Word of God and of the Body of the Lord" (CCC para.1346).

Prominent contemporary Catholic apologist Karl Keating, writing in *What Catholics Really Believe,* describes the Mass in the following manner:

> In the Mass the sacrifice of Calvary is 're-presented,' not in a bloody, physical way, but in an un-bloody, sacramental way. Christ's blood was shed only once, but it is continually offered to the Father. When a priest offers the sacrifice of the Mass, he is not offering a sacrifice distinct from that on Calvary. Christ is not dying all over again. What is on the altar is the very same sacrifice as on Calvary, but it is made present to us today in a special, sacramental way. This is a presence distinct from a physical, historical presence and distinct from a merely symbolic presence. It is a third kind of presence. In it Christ is really present on the altar, and at the consecration a real offering of Christ to the Father is made. Although Christ died only once, through the Mass his saving act is made actually present, day by day, until the end of time.

This "re-presentation," however, seems to be in conflict with statements from Vatican II (page 102), where the Catholic Church clearly states, "For in the sacrifice of the Mass Our Lord is immolated." Immolate, means "to kill" as a "sacrificial victim," according to Webster's Dictionary. Yet we know from the apostle Paul that, ". . . *Christ , once raised from the dead, will never die again; death has no more power over Him*" (Romans 6:9).

Keating, considered by many Catholic commentators as a modern day Archbishop Fulton J. Sheen, is very critical of his Catholic brothers and sisters saying, "The sad fact is that most Catholics, of all ages, are so poorly catechized that they can't explain to other Christians very much about their own faith. This shows especially in their discussion of the Mass. Their thinking is so hazy that they unknowingly concur with the Fundamentalist opponents of the Church"(*What Catholics Really Believe* – page 52). With Mr. Keating's complicated and somewhat confusing definition of the Mass, where he must invent "a third kind of presence," it is not surprising that many Catholic lay people are confused about what they are asked to believe.

Catholics Believe That the Sacrifice of the Mass is Identical with the Cross

The official position of the Catholic Church on the Mass was established at The Council of Trent in 1546, which declared, "The sacrifice [in the Mass] is identical with the sacrifice of the Cross, inasmuch as Jesus Christ is a priest and victim both." *The Q & A Catholic Catechism* by Hardon, S.J. (p. 256) says, "The mass, therefore, no less than the cross is atonement (satisfaction) for sins; but now the expiation (atonement) is experienced by those for whom, on the cross, the title of God's mercy had been gained." Christ is offered as a sacrifice for sins every time Mass is said, according to Catholic teaching.

The Catholic Encyclopedia defines the Liturgy of the Mass as follows: "The Mass is the complex of prayers and ceremonies that make up the service of the Eucharist in the Latin rites." Further in the Catholic Encyclopedia, it says, "from the time of the first preaching of the Christian faith in the West, as everywhere, the Holy Eucharist was celebrated as Christ had instituted it at the Last Supper."

The Catholic Mass is the central point of worship in the Catholic faith. It is a sacrifice (sacrifice of the mass), necessarily performed by a priest. If it is only a "re-presentation," as Keating suggests, why is a priest and altar necessary? There were no Christian priests in the first century church, because Christ "our high priest" had already gone to heaven to be with the Father. There was no priest at Calvary or the last supper, other than Christ! The preaching of the gospel (the homily) is relegated to a subordinate role in the ritual of the celebration of the Mass, with Communion—Eucharist as the integral part of the Mass.

Neither the Mass, a Christian sacrifice, nor a Christian priesthood, which would be necessary for the celebration of a "sacrifice of the Mass," is mentioned one time in all the pages of the New Testament. No ritual, celebration, or rite that would resemble the Mass, as defined by the Catholic Church, is found anywhere in the New Testament.

Some Catholic apologist point to the following verses in the Book of Malachi in the Old Testament, as a prophecy and description of the Catholic Mass, *"For from the rising of the sun, even to its setting, my name is great among the nations; And everywhere they bring sacrifice to my name, and a pure offering; For great is my name among the nations, says the Lord of hosts"* (Malachi 1:11). These verses, however, are clearly speaking of Israel, not Christianity. Malachi's zeal for Israel's sacrifices, coupled with his negative attitude toward foreigners and their gods (2:11; 3:2-5), points to the millennial era, when Israel will worship in the rebuilt temple, and incense plus offerings will be present (see Ezekiel 40-48). At that time, and not until that time, the Lord will receive pure worship throughout the world and His name will be honored everywhere.

The Book of Acts is a historical documentation of the activities of the early church. As mentioned earlier, Acts records the initial response to the Great Commission that Christ gave to the apostles before His ascension into heaven (Matthew 28:19, 20). The Book of Acts provides information on the first three decades of the church's existence. What was the church doing in those early years? The church was doing exactly what Christ instructed the apostles to do before His ascension: (1) Preaching the Gospel of Good News and Repentance (Acts 2:36, 37), and (2) Baptizing those that believed in the name of Jesus Christ (Acts 2:38). "*Those who accepted the message were baptized; some three thousand were added that day*" (Acts 2:41). "*They devoted themselves to the apostles' instructions and the communal life, to the breaking of bread and prayers*" (Acts 2:42).

Celebration of the Mass not Evident Anywhere in the New Testament

Nowhere in Acts do we find a priest celebrating the Mass, which is a distinct ritual needing an altar and a priest. Additionally, it would be highly unlikely that celebrating a Mass, which is not evangelical in nature, would have the result of saving three thousand souls, or five thousand souls, at one time. It is also important to note that in the Great Commission, found at the end of each of the three Synoptic Gospels, are Christ's final instructions to the apostles to preach the Gospel Good News and baptize those who believe. While the Lord's Supper was an important ordinance, it was not the centerpiece of Christianity, but preaching the gospel of repentance was. The Lord's Supper, while secondary to preaching the gospel and baptizing in Christ's economy, is clearly at the center of Catholic worship.

The early church was primarily Jewish, and they were continuing to use "God's house," the temple, for fellowship and prayer. "*They went to the temple area together each day, while in their homes they broke bread*" (Acts 2:46). In Acts 3:1, we read, "*Now Peter and John were going up to the temple at the ninth hour, the hour of prayer.*" The disciples went to the temple for the hours of prayer and, no doubt, to witness to others about the Good News. They had every right to use the temple, since Jesus had claimed it as His Father's house. They were still found going to the temple in Acts 21:26 and probably continued until it was destroyed in 70 A.D. To think that the Pharisees and other Jewish religious leaders, however, would allow the believers of "The Way" to celebrate a sacrifice of the Mass in the Jewish Temple or a synagogue would have been unthinkable.

The first Mass (Missa—Sacred Rite) was likely celebrated by Cyprian around A.D. 250 (after Polycarp and before Constantine). The Mass developed gradually as a sacrifice, and was made obligatory for all parishioners during the eleventh century. "In the beginning Mass was celebrated only once a week, then three or four times, and finally in the fifth or sixth century, every day" (Legislation on the Sacraments in the New Code of Canon Law, 87).

Trent declared that the Mass was a true and proper propitiatory sacrifice for sin made to God in a bloodless manner. But in John 19:30, Christ our Savior, cried out victoriously, "*Now it is finished.*" This one final act of a blood sacrifice completed once for all and continues in a state of completion. There is therefore, no need for further sacrifices. Christ was the final blood sacrifice for sin. The "un-bloody" sacrifice of the mass can never forgive sins, as is shown in Hebrews 9:22, "*According to the law almost everything is purified by blood, and without the shedding of blood there is no forgiveness.*" The sacrifice of the mass, therefore, does not qualify as a sin offering, and there is no need to continually offer Christ's blood to the Father, as Keating suggests, because Christ's work was finished.

Unlike the Other High Priests, Christ Has No Need to Offer Sacrifice Day after Day

The Bible clearly states that Christ was the final sacrifice and a perfect sacrifice. In 1 Peter 3:18 we read that, ". . . *Christ died for sins once for all. . . .*" Also in Hebrews 7:26, "*It was fitting that we should have such a high priest: holy, innocent, undefiled, separated from sinners, higher than the heavens. Unlike the other high priests, He has no need to offer sacrifice day after day, first for his own sins and then for those of the people; he did that once for all when he offered himself.*" Hebrews 10:10–14 reads, "*By this will we have been sanctified through the offering of the body of Jesus Christ once for all. And every priest stands daily ministering and offering time after time the same sacrifice, which can never take away sins; but He, having offered one sacrifice for sins for all time sat down at the right hand of God, waiting from that time onward until His enemies be made a footstool for His feet. For by one offering He has perfected for all time those who are sanctified.*" The Mass is a Catholic tradition that is in direct conflict with what the Scriptures state.

Scripture very clearly states that Christ paid the price for all of our sins on Calvary. The Bible does not say that Christ died for a certain type of sin, but for all sin. The sacrifice of the cross is a historical event. It occurred once, approximately 2,000 years ago, outside Jerusalem (Mark 15:21–41). This is the very reason that you see an empty cross when you enter a Protestant Church, since Protestants believe that Christ is in heaven sitting at the right hand of the Father, just as Scripture describes in Hebrews 10:12. Protestants are waiting for His Second Coming!

The Catholic Church has a crucifix in her churches because she believes that she is bringing Christ to thousands of altars each day by "re-presenting" over and over again the sacrifice of Christ to the Father (CCC para.1354, 1357), for sins that Protestants believe Christ has already died for on Calvary "once for all." God's love for us is minimized by the Catholic Church's position that Christ's sacrifice has to be continually repeated. To repeat the sacrifice of Jesus in the Mass would be to repeat his death. How can He die again since He is already seated at the right hand of the Father in heaven. "*Yes, God so loved the world that He gave His only*

Son, that whoever believes in Him may not die (shall not die—NASB) but have eternal life" (John 3:16).

The Catechism of the Catholic Church teaches, "For it is in the liturgy, especially in the Eucharist that the work of our redemption is accomplished" (CCC para. 1068).

The Bible tells us that in one act of supreme love, God paid the price for all of our sins, past, present, and future, and secured our redemption for eternity. God demanded justice for our sins, and Christ satisfied that demand for all mankind evermore. This was the gospel of "Good News!" Our job as Christians is to repent of our sins and follow God's plan for our lives as found in the Scriptures. Without Christ's sacrifice on Calvary, God would have to demand our death for justice for our sins! "*But now that you are free from sin and have become slaves of God, your benefit is sanctification as you tend toward eternal life. The wages of sin is death, but the gift of God is eternal life in Christ Jesus our Lord*" (Romans 6:22–23).

Further proof that the Mass and transubstantiation were not established or authorized by Christ at the Passover is found in Christ's final instructions to the disciples before He ascended into heaven. Christ's final instructions to the apostles are found in all three synoptic Gospels Matt. 28:16–20; Mark 16:15–16; Luke 24:44–49. We read in Mark, "*Go into all the world and proclaim the good news to all creation. The man believes in it and accepts baptism will be saved; the man who refuses to believe in it will be condemned.*" In

His significant final instructions to the disciples, Christ did not tell the apostles to go into the entire world and offer a daily sacrifice of the Mass. In His final instructions to the apostles there is also no mention of Christ saying anything about Communion, which is an integral part of Mass. Clearly, Communion (breaking of bread) was not meant to be the primary worship activity of the church.

In summary, the disciples followed these final instructions of Christ's, called by many the "Great Commission," after the ascension of Christ into heaven. They first preached the gospel of repentance, and then baptized those that believed, and celebrated Communion in remembrance of Christ's work on the cross. From the Book of Acts, which follows the Gospels, throughout the entire rest of the New Testament, finishing with the Book of Revelation, preaching or teaching is mentioned one hundred fifty-one times (151), Baptism forty-four times (44), but Communion is mentioned only fifteen times (15).

What was critical to Christianity was preaching the Gospel of repentance. There was no Christian priesthood to have a sacrifice of the Mass, and no activity that even remotely resembled the ritual of the Mass is mentioned in the New Testament. The sacrificial work of redemption was finished when Christ gave His life for us on the cross and said, "Now it is finished" (John 19:30).

Transubstantiation—The Catholic Catechism says, "The Council of Trent summarizes the Catholic faith by declaring: 'Because Christ our Redeemer said that it was truly his body that he was offering under the species of bread, it has always been the conviction of the Church of God, and this holy Council now declares again, that by the consecration of the bread and wine there takes place a change of the whole substance of the bread into the substance of the body of Christ our Lord and of the whole substance of the wine into the substance of his blood. This change the holy Catholic Church has fittingly and properly called transubstantiation'" (CCC para. 1376).

If not the most important doctrine of the Catholic Church, this is certainly one of the key doctrines and traditions of Catholicism. Transubstantiation is the foremost element in the celebration of the sacrifice of the Mass. The Catholic Church teaches that the whole substance of the bread and wine is changed into the literal, physical body and blood of Christ. The word "transubstantiation" means a change of substance. This philosophical concept was formulated into the doctrine of *Transubstantiation* and proclaimed by Pope Innocent II at the Fourth Lateran Council in 1215.

There are two main passages of Scripture that the Catholic Church uses in an attempt to prove this doctrine. The first is Jesus' words in the upper room: *This is My body* (Matthew 26:26), and *This is My blood of the covenant* (Matthew 26:28).

One might come along and say, If Jesus says that the bread and wine are His body and blood, who are we to say that He means they symbolize His body and blood? Are we not supposed to take His word literally?

The Lord's Supper

It is true that we are always supposed to accept the Word of God for what it says. The Bible is written in human languages, however, which have a definite grammar. All languages frequently use what are called figures of speech, expressions that by their very nature are obviously not meant to be taken literally. The accounts of the institution of the Lord's Supper, both in the Gospels and in Paul's letter to the Corinthians, make it perfectly clear that Christ spoke in figurative terms. Jesus said, "*This is the new covenant in My blood*" (Luke 22:20). Paul quotes Jesus as saying: ". . . *This cup is the new covenant in My blood. Do this, whenever you drink it, in remembrance of Me. Every time, then, when you eat this bread and drink this cup, you proclaim the death of the Lord until He comes*" (1 Cor.11:25–26). In these words he used a double figure of speech. The cup is used for the wine, and the wine is called the new covenant. The cup was not literally the new covenant, although it is declared to be so as definitely as the bread is declared to be His body. They did not literally drink the cup, nor did they literally drink the new covenant.

The most natural interpretation of Jesus' words is "this represents my body." If someone holds up a photograph, points to it, and says "This is me," the people around him will understand what he is saying. They would not suppose that he meant, "This photograph actually is my body. My body and blood are really present under the appearance of ink and paper." In fact they would not even entertain such an absurdity unless the one holding the picture explained himself to them. There is no record of any such explanation by the Lord Jesus. He simply held up the bread and said, "*This is My body*." That was all that was needed. The disciples understood what He meant. There was no implied miracle of Transubstantiation, and the disciples could not have missed the symbolic intent of Christ's statement, for His actual body was clearly right in front of them, and they could plainly see that it was not broken in any way.

On other occasions, Christ used similar language. He said, "*I am the sheep gate*" (John 10:7), but He did not mean that He was a literal sheep gate. Christ said, "*I am the vine*"

(John 15:5), but none understood Him to mean that he was an actual grapevine. When Christ said, "*Destroy this temple, and in three days I will raise it up*" (John 2:19), He meant His body, not the structure of wood and stone.

Catholics believe that a miracle occurs when the essence of the wafer (host) is claimed to be changed into the actual body and blood of Christ during Mass at the time of the consecration (transubstantiation), even though the wafer continues to look and taste exactly the same as it did before. In the Bible, however, all of the miracles performed by Christ included dramatic visual evidence that proved the validity of the miracle. In John 2:1, the water at the marriage feast in Cana of Galilee was actually changed physically into the finest wine, and unlike the communion wafer, it did not remain under the appearance of water. In other biblical miracles Christ restored life to the dead son of a nobleman (John 4), Christ healed the paralytic, and he picked up his pallet and walked (John 5), Christ feeds five thousand with five barley loaves and two fish, and had twelve baskets of barley loaves and fish left over (John 6), Christ heals the man blind from birth, and he could see (John 9), Christ raises Lazarus from the dead, after he had been in the tomb for four days (John 11). In each case it was clear to all who witnessed these miracles of Christ that in fact they were true miracles and occurred exactly as written in the Word of God.

Christ's words, "*This do in remembrance of Me*" show that the Lord's Supper was not some sort of mystical event, but primarily a memorial, instituted to call Christians throughout the ages to remember the wondrous cross of the crucified Lord and all of its marvelous benefits and lessons for us. In many ways, the importance of the ritual of the Mass in the Catholic faith parallels the critical importance of preaching the Gospel of repentance and teaching its principles in the Protestant faith.

The second passage of Scripture the Roman Catholic Church uses in trying to defend the doctrine of transubstantiation is John 6:53–55: "*Jesus said to them, 'Amen, amen, I say to you, unless you eat the flesh of the Son of man and drink his blood, you do not have life within you. Whoever eats my flesh and drinks my blood has eternal life, and I will raise him on the last day. For my flesh is true food, and my blood is true drink.*'"

Catholics take it for granted that these words of Jesus were uttered in connection with the Last Supper. This is not the case! The context of John 6:51–53 was Christ's preaching in the synagogue at Capernum some days after the miracle of feeding the 5,000, long before the experiences of the Last Supper in the upper room, which would come two years later. His audience in the synagogue at Capernum was mostly unbelieving Jews. The eating of His flesh and the drinking of His blood metaphorically symbolized the need for accepting Jesus' work on the cross. Jesus' reference here to eating and drinking was not referring to the ordinance of communion for two reasons: 1) Communion had not been instituted yet, and 2) If Jesus was referring to communion the passage would teach that anyone partaking of communion would receive eternal life.

It is puzzling that while the Catholic Church takes Christ's words in Matthew 26 very literally, "*Take this and eat it* (bread)...*this is my body*," and "*All of you must drink from it* (cup)...*this is My blood*," yet in actual practice the

Catholic Church today only follows half of Christ's instructions. In the vast majority of Masses celebrated around the world each day only the Catholic priest himself actually eats both the bread and drinks the wine. The parishioners only have the opportunity to consume the bread (host), and are not given the opportunity to drink of the cup. In contrast Protestant Churches celebrating the Lord's Supper offer the congregation both the bread to eat and the fruit of the vine to drink, as Christ instructed.

Christ Ascends into Heaven and Sends the Holy Spirit

Scriptures tell us that when Christ ascended into heaven to sit at the right hand of the Father until the Second Coming, He sent the Holy Spirit, the Third Person of the Trinity, to take His place. "*Yet I tell you the sober truth: It is much better for you that I go. If I fail to go the Paraclete (Comforter—Holy Spirit) will never come to you, whereas if I go, I will send Him to you*" (John 16:7). It is inconsistent with Scripture, therefore, to say that Christ, who sits at the right hand of the Father waiting on the Second Coming, would be "actually present" in the host of the Eucharist as the Catholic Church claims, thereby usurping the role that God gave to the Holy Spirit in our lives today. It is clear from Christ's words that Christ and the Holy Spirit have separate roles in our redemption and sanctification. It would make more theological sense to say that the Holy Spirit is in the Eucharist, not Christ, but that would not be correct either. Christ fulfilled His role on earth with His ascension into heaven, but He then sent the Holy Spirit to take His place until His Second Coming. Christ told the apostles, and by extension each of us, "*This much I have told you while I was still with you: the Paraclete, the Holy Spirit, whom the Father will send in My name, will instruct you in everything and remind you of all that I told you. Peace is My farewell to you, My peace is My gift to you; I do not give it to you as the world gives peace. Do not be distressed or fearful. You have heard me say 'I go away for a while, and I come back to you (Second Coming).' If you truly loved Me you would rejoice to have Me go to the Father, for the Father is greater than I*" (John 14:25–28). We are not filled with "Christ," per se, we are filled with the "Holy Spirit."

Worship of the Consecrated Host or the Blessed Sacrament

Finally, the Catholic Catechism says that God desires that the consecrated bread and wine be worshiped as divine, with the following quote:

"*Worship of the Eucharist*. In the liturgy of the mass we express our faith in the real presence of Christ under the species of bread and wine by, among other ways, genuflecting or bowing deeply as a sign of adoration of the Lord. 'The Catholic Church has always offered and still offers to the sacrament of the Eucharist the cult of adoration, not only during

Mass, but also outside of it, reserving the consecrated hosts with the utmost care, exposing them to the solemn veneration of the faithful, and carrying them in procession'" (CCC para. 1378).

The Catholic Church's list of the 10 Commandments revises the original Second Commandment that refers to idolatry; "*You shall have no other gods before Me. You shall not make for yourself a graven image, or any likeness of anything that is in heaven above, or that is in the earth beneath, or that is in the water under the earth,*" thereby eliminating the original Second Commandment and lessening its emphasis and the church splits the tenth Commandment into the ninth; "*You shall not covet your neighbor's wife,*" and the tenth; "*You shall not covet your neighbor's goods,*" to arrive at her own revised list of 10 Commandments. (CCC page 496–497)

In the Bible, God forbids the worship of any object, even those intended to represent Him. In Exodus 20:4, 5, we read, " *You shall not carve idols for yourselves in the shape of anything in the sky above or the earth below or in the waters beneath the earth; you shall not bow down before them or worship them.*" In Isaiah 42:8, we read, "*I am the Lord, this is My name; my glory I give to no other, nor My praise to idols;" and in the New Testament Jesus said, "God is Spirit, and those who worship Him must worship in Spirit (which is invisible) and truth*" (John 4:24). Clearly the communion wafer (host) is not the Holy Spirit, and must not be worshipped.

The Inquisition—It would be impossible to examine any Roman Catholic historical evolution without some mention of the Roman Catholic Inquisition. In his book, *Why Catholicism Matters*, author and President of the Catholic League, Bill Donohue, attempts to minimize the Catholic Church's involvement in the horrors of the Inquisition. Donohue, writing about the Inquisition states, "Most of what is related in the grossly exaggerated tales of horrors never happened, and in any event the secular authorities, not the Catholic Church were at the center of events. The source of the many anti-Catholic myths is not in doubt; they stem from the 'Black Legend' writings that were disseminated in the aftermath of the Protestant Reformation. The propaganda against Catholicism continues today, although these days the source is academia."

The truth is that the Inquisition was the Catholic Church's Court for the detection and punishment of heretics. Everyone was required by law to inform against heretics. Anyone suspected of heresy was subject to torture or death, without knowing the name of his or her accuser. The proceedings were secret. The Inquisitor pronounced the sentence, and the victim was turned over to the civil authorities for harsh punishment such as torture, imprisonment for life, or burning at the stake. The victim's property was confiscated and divided between the Church and the State.

In *A Brief History of The Inquisition,* author Robert Jones writes, "The methods of the Inquisition were also given blessing from the most renowned Catholic theologians of the time, as the following startling passages from Saint Thomas Aquinas' (1225–1274 A.D.) massive theological work *Summa Theologica* show. Aquinas, a Dominican monk, is generally considered to be the greatest Catholic theologian since Augustine in the 4/5 centuries—and Aquinas talks of the extermination of heretics:

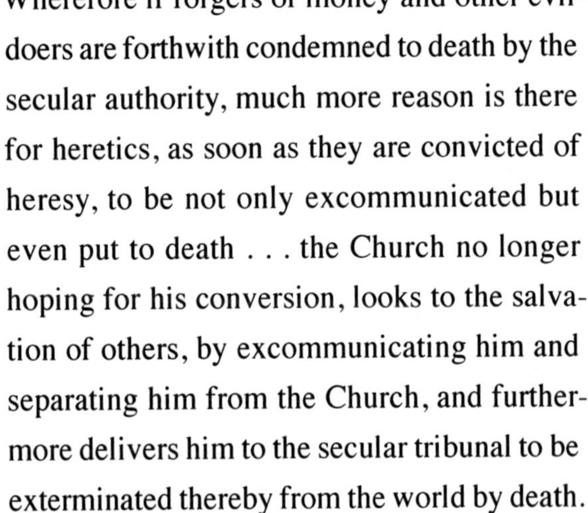

> Wherefore if forgers of money and other evil-doers are forthwith condemned to death by the secular authority, much more reason is there for heretics, as soon as they are convicted of heresy, to be not only excommunicated but even put to death . . . the Church no longer hoping for his conversion, looks to the salvation of others, by excommunicating him and separating him from the Church, and furthermore delivers him to the secular tribunal to be exterminated thereby from the world by death. (Summa Theologica—Vol. 3 – The Second Part of the Second Part (Part I), p. 150.

The Inquisition labeled Christians who did not believe in transubstantiation or other Catholic doctrines as heretics, and while exact numbers are not available, it is clear that hundreds of thousands, if not millions, were cruelly tortured or slaughtered in over six hundred and fifty years of Catholic Inquisitions from the Episcopal Inquisition of November 4, 1184, to the end of the Spanish Inquisition on July 15, 1834. Catholic apologists, such as Donohue, like to point out that it was the state that actually put heretics to death, but Dollinger, who was the leading nineteenth century Catholic historian said, "The binding force of the laws against heretics lay not in the authority of secular princes, but in the sovereign dominion of life and death over all Christians claimed by the popes as God's representatives on earth."

Philip De Courcy, in his book *Standing Room Only*, recounts one of the thousands of tragic stories of the Catholic Inquisition:

> Nineteen year-old William Hunter refused an edict to attend Mass and receive the Communion because 'it would be sin against God to countenance such idolatries.' His confession was that 'he was in heart and soul a Protestant and dared not in conscience attend the Mass.' He was encouraged to persevere in his stand by his parents; 'I am glad my son,' said his mother, 'that God has given me such a child, who can find it in his heart to lose his

life for Christ's sake.' Hunter died in the fire at Brentwood in Essex in March 1555.

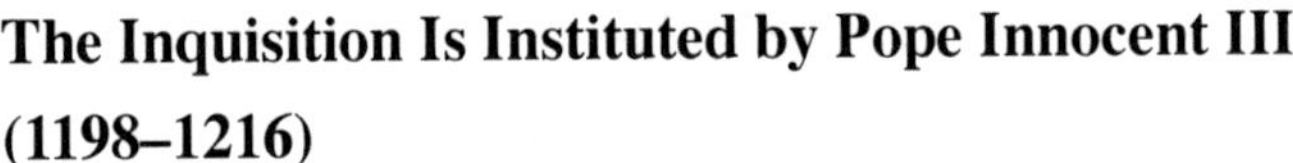

The Inquisition Is Instituted by Pope Innocent III (1198–1216)

The Inquisition, called the "Holy Office," was officially instituted by Pope Innocent III (1198–1216) and was perfected under Pope Gregory IX (1227–1241) and Pope Boniface VIII, who in 1302 issued the *Unam Sanctam,* a document in which he claimed to be the representative of God on earth and concurrently claimed authority over every nation and government on earth. According to most historians, the Inquisition was the most infamous event in history. When the Spanish Inquisition was abolished, a Spanish historian recorded that no fewer than 340,000 persons, had been judged and punished of whom at least 32,000 were burned alive, among them the flower of Spanish nobility who had embraced the primitive Gospel. Torquemada, a Dominican friar and priest, was alone responsible for 8,800 deaths by fire. In the Massacre of St. Bartholomew in 1572, more than 5,000 Huguenots were imprisoned and murdered by the Roman Catholic Chateaubriand, in five days. The killings extended to all of France and lasted two months. Seventy thousand were assassinated, according to historians.

One reformer who died in Germany was a Bohemian Catholic priest named John Hus. He believed that people should be permitted to read the Bible in their own language. He was condemned at the Council of Constance, burned at the stake in 1415, and his ashes were thrown into the Rhine. Martin Luther would have been martyred had the local German ruler, Frederick III (the Wise), not refused to hand Luther over to the pope. Pope Alexander III excommunicated Peter Waldo for declaring that the Bible was the only source of truth and commanded the bishop to "exterminate all the Waldenses, if possible, on the face of the earth." In France, Peter Chapot, was burned at the stake in 1546 for bringing a number of Bibles in the French tongue to France to distribute. William Tyndale was strangled and burned at the stake in 1536 in Belgium for translating the Bible into English. One could fill books with other examples of such Inquisition horrors.

Over the centuries many Catholics have criticized Martin Luther for not trying to reform the Catholic Church from within. Author, Michael Thomsett reports, however, that "The ideas in Luther's dissertation (95 Theses) were intended as the starting point for internal reform, and not as a confrontation or challenge to the Church. He sent this document in a letter of October 31, 1517, to Albrecht, archbishop of Mainz and Magdeburg, and to Wittenberg's own bishop, Hieronymus Scultetus" (*The Inquisition: A History*).

The Catholic Church Evolves from a Religion into an Authoritarian World Power

How did the Catholic Church evolve from a peaceful ideology centered in Christ alone in the early fourth century to a world power that would dominate both world religion and world politics by the end of the first millennium? The church felt threatened as many were being identified as heretics, and in response the church became more and more aligned with the power and resources of the Roman Empire as the Catholic Church began to dominate nations of the world. With this Roman Empire power at her disposal, Pope Innocent III instituted the Inquisition, to deal with fallen-away Catholics and others that would not convert to Catholicism. Thomsett writes:

> The point of view that heresy and other crimes against God or the Church deserved a death sentence, and not just excommunication, emerged around the end of the 4th century. From the early Church and its initial temporal tolerance of heresy, changes in opinion led, over the course of some 1,000 years, to the founding of the Inquisition (from the Latin *inquiro,* to inquire) as a permanent church-based judicial institution. Originally based on the search for heretics, alchemists, and

> witches, the Inquisition system soon became useful as a means for punishing political enemies or seizing land and wealth. Punishments varied over time based on the approach of individual inquisitors and guidelines from various popes (*The Inquisition: A History*).

Thomsett felt that the genesis of the Inquisition had to be studied historically with a progressing attitude that might evolve over the six and a half centuries of Catholic Inquisitions. Thomsett's view was that no Inquisition was likely to appear without it first being rationalized in church doctrine and belief. The first century church was made up of independent congregations that likely met in various Christian homes, where this evolution would be unlikely. From the time of Constantine, however, the idea of a single institutional church was promoted, and became reality in A.D. 380, when Emperor Theodosius declared Roman Catholic Christianity the Roman Empire state religion.

This decision granted great power to Christianity, which from that point forward was known as the *Roman* Church, protected by the wealth and military might of the Empire. It also transformed the spiritual church into a temporal power.

Thomsett summarizes; "Thus, the Inquisition was the offspring of the union of Church and State in the single entity of the Holy Roman Empire. Given the power inherent in this union, it is easy to understand how the Inquisition grew and expanded."

Protestant Inquisition

History tells us that, even after nearly four hundred years of Inquisition horrors, perpetrated by the Catholic Church on those that did not agree with Catholic teachings, that once Protestants accomplished the religious freedom they desired, many turned on Catholic minorities in Protestant countries. In Germany and Switzerland, properties owned by Catholic orders were seized and their occupants banished, sent to prison, and some even murdered. Only Lutheran services were allowed in Norway and Denmark, and it became a crime under Elizabeth I to practice any religion except Anglicanism in England.

Protestants might say that after nearly four hundred years of Catholic Inquisition, that their actions were a matter of "an eye for an eye, and a tooth for a tooth" (Exodus 21:24), and were justified as acts of righteous indignation. They might even say that the number of Catholics persecuted were small in number and for a relatively brief period of history. The problem with this kind of reasoning, however, was that the Catholics they were persecuting were not the same individuals at whose hands Protestants had been tortured and killed in the past centuries. Additionally, had they not read Romans 12:19, "*Beloved, do not avenge yourselves; leave that to God's wrath, for it is written: 'VENGEANCE IS MINE, I WILL REPAY,' says the Lord?*" Protestants proved that they were just as capable of the satanic evil of persecuting innocents as their Catholic transgressors had been, and by their actions demonstrated that the Protestant Church, per se, also failed to meet "The One True Church" test of Matthew 16:18. Author Jones writes, "However, as an institution, the Catholic Inquisition stands alone in terms of the length of time it existed, the number of its victims, the ruthlessness of its methodologies, and the intolerance that it fostered" *(A Brief History of The Inquisition*).

It is also clear from internal documents of the Catholic Church herself that confiscation of property was a major objective of the Inquisition, creating immense wealth for the church. In an article on the Inquisition in the Catholic Encyclopedia we read the following: "They caused many citizens in their domains, nobles and commoners, clerics, knights, peasants, spinsters, widows, and married women, to be burnt alive, confiscated their property, and divided it between them (church and state)" (Catholic Encyclopedia, VIII 29).

Thomsett writes, "Even with its condemnation of torture, the Catholic Church never abolished the Supreme sacred Congregation of the Roman and Universal Inquisition. On December 7, 1965, Pope Paul VI issued the bull *Integrae Servandae,* officially renaming the Inquisition office the Sacred Congregation for the Doctrine of the Faith

(*Congregatio pro Doctrina Fidei*, or CDF). Today, this is the longest-standing office of the Roman Curia" (*The Inquisition: A History*).

Finally, in the year 2000, after more than one hundred and fifty years since the abolishment of the Spanish Inquisition, Pope John Paul II officially apologized to the world for the atrocities of the Inquisition perpetrated on individuals suspected of being in conflict with Catholic Church teaching:

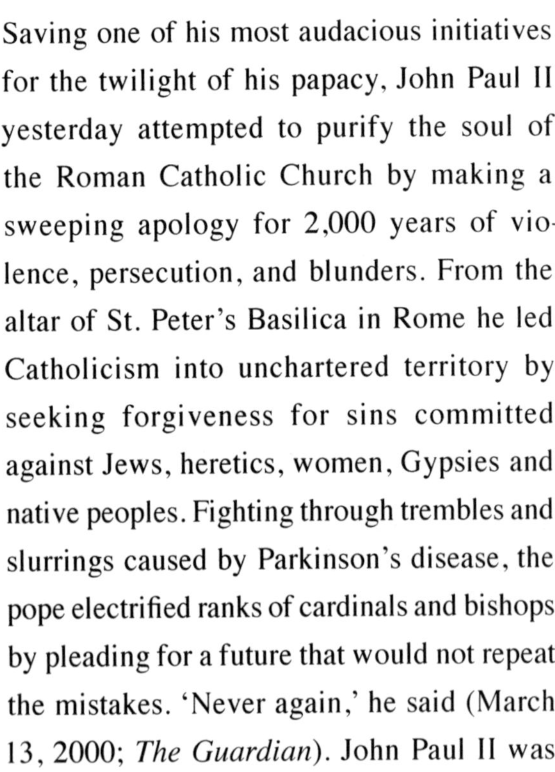

> Saving one of his most audacious initiatives for the twilight of his papacy, John Paul II yesterday attempted to purify the soul of the Roman Catholic Church by making a sweeping apology for 2,000 years of violence, persecution, and blunders. From the altar of St. Peter's Basilica in Rome he led Catholicism into unchartered territory by seeking forgiveness for sins committed against Jews, heretics, women, Gypsies and native peoples. Fighting through trembles and slurrings caused by Parkinson's disease, the pope electrified ranks of cardinals and bishops by pleading for a future that would not repeat the mistakes. 'Never again,' he said (March 13, 2000; *The Guardian*). John Paul II was

canonized as a saint of the Roman Catholic Church on April 27, 2014.

Christian Priesthood—The Catechism says the following about the Catholic priesthood: "'It is in the Eucharistic cult or in the Eucharistic assembly of the faithful (*synaxis*) that they (priests) exercise in a supreme degree their sacred office; there, acting in the person of Christ and proclaiming His mystery, they unite the votive offerings of the faithful to the sacrifice of Christ their head, and in the sacrifice of the Mass they make present again and apply, until the coming of the Lord, the unique sacrifice of the New Testament, that namely of Christ offering Himself once for all a spotless victim to the Father.' From this unique sacrifice their whole priestly ministry draws its strength" (CCC para. 1566).

It is not surprising that we find no mention of the Christian priesthood or an altar in a church in all of the New Testament. If there was no sacrifice of the Mass, then there was no need of a priesthood or an altar. The Jewish and pagan priesthoods that are mentioned in the Bible were common only in that they offered sacrifices. The Jewish priesthood existed primarily to offer sacrifices to God for sin on behalf of the people, and taught the people the law of God, but disappeared once the Jewish temple was destroyed in A.D. 70. The priesthood that came later in the Catholic Church would evolve over time. It was not until the third and fourth centuries that priests began to appear in the Catholic Church as the sacrifice of the Mass became a tradition.

The Greek word for priest in both Old and New Testaments is *hiereus*, which means sacred or consecrated person, set apart for God's service. This term should not be confused with the word *presbyteros*, which means elder, senior people to whom leadership was entrusted. The apostle Peter, an apostle and a church leader, spoke of himself as a "*fellow presbyter*" (*presbyteros* or elder), but never as a priest, *hiereus* (1 Peter 5:1).

Paul enumerates the different kinds of ministers and agents in the Christian church, and the office of the priest is not among them: "*And God hath set some in the church, first apostles, secondly prophets, thirdly teachers . . .*" (1 Cor.12:28). There is never any mention of priests. The description of a Presbyter (a teaching elder) in the book of Titus would certainly not characterize a Roman Catholic priest of today. "*A Presbyter must be irreproachable, married only once, the father of children who are believers and are known not to be wild and insubordinate*" (Titus 1:6). In Paul's Epistle to the Ephesians, 4:11–12, Paul says, "*It is He who gave apostles, prophets, evangelists, pastors, and teachers in roles of service for the faithful to build up the body of Christ.*" Once again, there is no mention of priests.

No Christian Priesthood in the New Testament

In the Epistle to the Hebrews, the writer devotes several chapters to explaining that the Old Testament priesthood has been abolished and that there is no place in Christianity for a sacrificing priesthood because Christ, "*through His own blood, entered in once for all into the holy place, having obtained eternal redemption*," *and He has offered* "*one sacrifice for sins for eve*r" (Hebrews 9:12; 10:12). Peter writes to the church, "*You, however, are 'a chosen race, a royal priesthood, a holy nation, a people He claims for His own to proclaim the glorious works of the One who called you from darkness into His marvelous light*" (1 Peter 2:9).

All born-again believers, having now been given access to God through Christ their Savior, and being able to go directly to God in prayer and to intercede for themselves and others, have become priests of God. For these are the activities of a priest. This Christians call *the universal priesthood of believers*. And this is the distinctive feature of Protestantism regarding the doctrine of the priesthood.

We read in Matthew 23:9, "*Do not call anyone on earth your father. Only one is your father, the one in heaven.*" In this passage Christ is forbidding the use of titles such as Rabbi and father, to be used in a sense that accords undue spiritual authority to a human being, as if he were the source of truth rather than God. In spite of this admonition the Catholic

Church requires Catholics to call the pope "Holy Father," and Catholics to address priests as "father."

The Catholic Church made her church leaders into priests and by definition have taken the God-given privileges of priesthood away from the believer. The Catholic priest stands between God and His people whom He (Christ) reconciled. The veil in the temple that God tore from top to bottom when Jesus died on the cross at Calvary, the Catholic Church has repaired and put back in place.

The following Scriptures were written after the Apostles were sent forth to preach the Gospel and much earlier than the day Roman Catholic teachers insisted Christ made Peter the head of His Church. Clearly, therefore, the early Christians did not look upon any of the apostles as "another Christ" or regard them as mediators:

* "To Jesus, the mediator of a new covenant, and to the sprinkled blood which speaks more eloquently than that of Abel" (Hebrews 12: 24).
* "For through Him we both have access in one Spirit to the Father" (Ephesians 2:18).
* "Now that we have been justified by faith, we are at peace with God through our Lord Jesus Christ" (Romans 5:1, 2).
* "God is one, One also is the mediator between God and men, the man Christ Jesus, who gave as a ransom for all" (1 Timothy 2:5).

Celibacy/Priesthood Abuses—The Catechism of the Catholic Church says, "All the ordained ministers of the Latin Church, with the exception of permanent deacons, are normally chosen from among men of faith who live a celibate life and who intend to remain *celibate* "for the sake of the kingdom of heaven." Called to consecrate themselves with undivided heart to the Lord and to "the affairs of the Lord," they give themselves entirely to God and to men. Celibacy is a sign of this new life to the service of which the Church's minister is consecrated; accepted with a joyous heart celibacy radiantly proclaims the Reign of God" (CCC para. 1579).

The Roman Catholic Church officially imposed celibacy on all priests in the eleventh century (1079 A.D.). Although many monastics practiced celibacy prior to that time, there was no law forbidding the clergy to be married. Several popes, many bishops, and very many priests were married men. Most of the twelve disciples, including Peter, were married men.

Catholic seminaries have taught that several things led to the decision to forbid the clergy to marry: rampant immorality in Catholic families, married priests breaking the "seal of secrecy" by telling their wives what they had heard in the confessional, and fear of losing church property to the children of priests. But the greatest reason for the decision was a Gnostic philosophy embraced by theologians in the Middle Ages, which taught that "the soul is basically good, while the flesh is fundamentally evil." This false assumption led to the conviction that sexual activity was a "necessary evil for the propagation of mankind." Since sexual activity is substantially evil, those who have been called to serve God as His priests, to be endowed with great supernatural powers, should not be involved with this activity.

Priestly celibacy has left an undeniable scar of abuse over centuries on the Catholic Church. Historian William Manchester, in his portrait of an age, *A World Lit Only by Fire,* gives us a glimpse of the impact of Catholic Church celibacy in the Middle Ages. Of that age in history, Manchester writes, "Now celibacy yielded to widespread clerical concubinage and, in the convents and homes for fatherless, children were born to women who had pledged their virtue as brides of Christ."

Manchester continues:

> The precept that men of God should sleep alone, established by the Lateran Councils of 1123 and 1139 after nine hundred years of dawdling, and had begun to fray well before the dawn of the sixteenth century. Now it was a thing of shreds and patches. The last pontiff to take it seriously had died in 1471 (Pope Paul II), and even he, during his youthful days as

> bishop of Trieste, had assignations with a succession of mistresses. A generation later the occupants of Saint Peter's chair were openly acknowledging their bantlings, endowing their sons with titles and their daughters with dowries.

Another abuse of the priesthood reported by Manchester was that Pope Innocent VIII, who succeeded Pope Sixtus IV in 1484, raised simony to new levels to support the life style of Franceschetto Cibo, his son by a nameless courtesan. "By the time he found a suitable bride for Franceschetto, a Medici, he had to mortgage the papal tiara and treasury to pay for the wedding. Then he appointed his son's new brother-in-law to the Sacred College. The new cardinal and future Pope Leo X was fourteen years old."

Catholic Church Settles Largest Lawsuit in Priestly Abuses for $660 Million

The Catholic Church herself revealed that there have been over 13,000 credible sexual abuse accusations against Catholic clerics in the U.S. between 1950 and 2007. *The Los Angeles Times* headline story on July 15, 2007, read, "$660-MILLION SETTLEMENT IN PRIEST ABUSES—L.A. Archdiocese's payout to 508 claimants is the largest sex scandal that has rocked the

Catholic Church." This settlement brought the total payout for the Los Angeles Archdiocese alone to some $774 million dollars since 2002, which includes over 570 claimants. This was closely followed by a $198 million settlement by the Diocese of San Diego. Nationally, this brought the total cost-to-date (9/07) of settlements for the Catholic Church sex abuse cases since 1950 to $2.3 billion dollars. The problem is pervasive in the United States, with huge settlements in Boston; Portland; Covington, Kentucky; San Francisco; Orange County, California; and Tucson, as well as many other dioceses. It is of interest to note, however, that The Archdiocese of Los Angeles reportedly has insurance coverage and owns some $4 billion of real estate that could be used to cover her exposure.

In response to the above settlement in Los Angeles, the Vatican's chief spokesman, Father Federico Lombardi, stated, "Other organized religions and institutions should also deal with pedophilia as publicly as the Catholic Church has been forced to by various scandals." He also said, "The problem of the abuse of childhood and its adequate protection does not regard only the (Catholic) Church, but also many other institutions, and it is right that these take the necessary decisions as by various scandals." There seems to be a sense among many Catholics and others that all religions and institutions have similar levels of sexual abuse. That the church claiming to be The One True Church should be the example of morality to the rest, and not the subject of immorality, appears to have been lost on Catholics at the Vatican and across the United States.

Levels of Sex Claims against Minors Much Higher in Catholic Clergy

While it is clear that sin is ubiquitous among all men, including Protestant clergy, the facts do not support the notion among some Catholics that Protestant clergy have similar, if not higher, levels of sex scandal claims against minors. The fact is that 54 percent of Americans claim to be Protestant. On June 14, 2007, the Associated Press reported that the three insurance companies that insure the majority of Protestant churches in the United States said that they received upward of 260 reports each year of young people under 18 being sexually abused by Protestant clergy, church staff, or congregation members. These companies insure 171,000 clients that are clergy and church staff in 165,495 Protestant churches in the United States. Statistically, this works out to 0.2 percent of Protestant clergy or church staff being accused of sexual abuse, which is certainly to be condemned.

In comparison, 24 percent of Americans claim to be Roman Catholic. In 2006, according to official Catholic sources (U.S. Conference of Catholic Bishops), there were 714 new allegations against diocesan clergy (783 in 2005, and 1092 in 2004). There are 19,000 Catholic parishes in the United States with 46,000 priests. Statistically this works out to 1.6 percent of Catholic priests being accused of sexual abuse, or conservatively, eight times higher on average, than Protestant clergy. It would be even higher if only Protestant clergy were compared, rather than including church staff and even the congregation in the numbers.

Priest Abuse a Worldwide Problem for the Catholic Church

While there may be many reasons for the high percentage of sexual abuse incidents among the clergy in the Catholic Church, clearly celibacy appears to be a large contributing factor. The Apostle Paul's thoughts on forbidding marriage are expressed clearly in 1 Tim 4:1–5: "*The Spirit distinctly says that in later times some will turn away from the faith (they never truly had it) and will heed deceitful spirits and things taught by demons through plausible liars—men with seared consciences who forbid marriage and require abstinence from foods which God created to be received with thanksgiving by believers who know the truth.*" False teachers in Ephesus were forbidding marriage, but Paul reminded Timothy that marriage was created by God and is therefore good. Neither celibacy nor any form of diet saves or sanctifies. In First Corinthians, Chapter 7, Paul confirms that marriage is not a sin, and it is better to marry than to burn with passion.

It should be noted that the problem of sexual abuse in the Catholic Church is not only pervasive in the United States; it is a problem for the Catholic Church worldwide. In May of 2006, Pope Benedict XVI asked the founder of the Legion of Christ, Mexican priest Marcial Maciel, to stop celebrating public Masses after allegations that he sexually abused seminarians. In October of 2006, Pope Benedict told a group of bishops from Ireland that, "It is urgent to rebuild confidence and trust" in an overwhelmingly Catholic country where all seminaries but one have closed following repeated scandals.

By April of 2010, the sex-abuse scandal among Catholic priests had reached crisis proportions globally, with major new scandals surfacing in Malta, Germany, Austria, Netherlands, Ireland, Belgium, Mexico, and the United States. The scandals reaching even Pope Benedict himself coming under "particular scrutiny for his handling of abusive priests when he was archbishop of Munich-Freising, in the late 1970s and early 1980s, and then as head of the Congregation for the Doctrine of the Faith, a Vatican office that reviewed some cases of sexual abuse" (WSJ 4/16/10). "In an investigation spanning 21 countries across six continents, The Associated Press found 30 cases of priests accused of abuse who were transferred or moved abroad. Some escaped police investigation. Many had access to children in another country, and some abused again" (AP 4/18/10).

Pope Benedict Calls on Catholic Church to Take Responsibility for Her Scandals

On May 11, 2010, "Pope Benedict XVI called on the Roman Catholic Church to take responsibility for its crisis of sexual-abuse allegations against priests dismissing claims that the scandal had been whipped up in order to discredit the church. 'The greatest persecution of the church doesn't come from enemies on the outside but is born from the sin within the church,' Pope Benedict said, according to Vatican radio. Responding to a question about the 'suffering' of the church amid allegation of sexual abuse of minors, the pontiff placed the blame for the scandal squarely on the church and called for 'purification'" (WSJ 5/12/10).

To her credit, "The Vatican launched an investigation into whether seven priests in the Legion of Christ sexually abused minors, the Vatican and Legion said . . . opening a new chapter in the prominent religious order's struggle to recover from a scandal that disgraced its founder . . . Father Marcial Maciel, who denied the allegations, died in 2008, before the Vatican definitely concluded an investigation" (WSJ—5/12/14).

First Catholic Priest Convicted and Imprisoned

A Philadelphia jury handed down the first high-level conviction of an American Catholic priest on June 22, 2012. "Msgr. William Lynn, who served as secretary for clergy in the archdiocese of Philadelphia from 1992 to 2004, was found guilty on Friday of one count of child endangerment for allowing a priest to take a new assignment involving contact with children even after learning of allegations that he had engaged in inappropriate contact with at least one minor" (WSJ 6/23/12). Father Lynn was sentenced to six years in prison. After serving eighteen months, a Pennsylvania appeals court overturned the conviction of Msgr. Lynn for insufficient evidence to link him directly to child endangerment. The church and victims are closely watching this case, as the District Attorney plans to appeal the decision according to a WSJ article of December 27, 2013.

It must be said, however, that alongside priests who are caught up in sexual scandal are the majority of Catholic priests, who are sincere, trying to be faithful to God, and silently suffering the humiliation of association. These well-intended men are forgotten by the media, who focus on evil as opposed to their good works, in trying to serve God in the way they have been instructed by the Catholic Church. It would be foolish for non-Catholic professing Christians to think that somehow their religious leaders are immune from sexual abuses, as is shown in the above statistics. Even with the advantage of not having celibacy to deal with and the added benefit that most non-Catholic pastors are accountable to their own congregation locally, sexual abuse is still reported. Modern history is replete with the names of preachers accused of sexual scandals: Jim Bakker, Jimmy

Swaggart, Bishop Clarence McClendon, Paul Crouch (TBN), and Ted Haggart, among others. Many of these sex offenders come out of the charismatic "health, wealth, and prosperity gospel movement which is clearly unbiblical but has unfortunately become the face of Christianity in the media.

There is great hope both inside and outside the Catholic Church, that Pope Francis, who is showing himself to be a reformer, will take a fresh look at celibacy, and put in place strict reforms that will lessen the opportunity for these kinds of abuses to occur in the Catholic Church in the future. On September 12, 2013, the Vatican Secretary of State announced that celibacy was now "open for review" (Yahoo! News). Additionally, according to the Vatican, "Pope Francis will establish a special commission to help advise the Catholic Church on how to better handle the problem of sexual abuse of children, one of the first big moves to confront an issue that has badly shaken the church" (WSJ 12/6/13).

Vatican Disciplined 3,420 Catholic Priests for Abuse of Minors Over Nine Years

Finally, the Vatican disclosed that it had defrocked 848 priests and had given lesser punishments to 2,572 priests for sexual abuse of minors from 2004 to 2013, as it sought to demonstrate to a United Nations panel, on May 6, 2014, its commitment to tackle a scandal that has shaken the church. Members of Pope Francis' newly appointed Pontifical

Commission for the Protection of Minors hope to consolidate the practice of holding bishops or other supervisors accountable for priests who abuse children under their watch. All of this was in response to a February 2014 charge by a U.N. Committee on the Rights of the Child that "criticized the Vatican for focusing more on shielding the members of the clergy than on protecting the victims in its response to the sexual-abuse cases, which the committee had numbered in the "tens of thousands" (*Wall Street Journal*—5/7/14). In its final statement on the above charge, the United Nations committee members "welcomed guidelines issued by the Vatican's disciplinary body instructing church authorities to cooperate with civil authorities, but expressed concern that they continued to 'resist the principle of mandatory reporting.' The committee cited the case of Archbishop Paul Gallagher, the papal envoy to Australia who invoked diplomatic immunity last year in refusing to provide documents that could assist a commission of inquiry into sex abuse" (*New York Times*, May 24, 2014).

The Papacy—The Catechism tells us, "The Pope, Bishop of Rome and Peter's successor, 'is the perpetual and visible source and foundation of the unity both of the bishops and of the whole company of the faithful.' 'For the Roman Pontiff, by reason of his office as Vicar of Christ, and as pastor of the entire Church has full, supreme, and universal power over the whole Church, a power which he can always exercise unhindered'" (CCC para. 882). "'The college or body of bishops has no authority unless united with the Roman Pontiff, Peter's successor, as its head.' As such, this college has 'supreme and full authority over the universal Church; but this power cannot be exercised without the agreement of the Roman Pontiff'" (CCC para. 883).

During the time of the apostles and their disciples, the earliest church fathers of the Christian era knew nothing of any spiritual supremacy on the part of the bishops of Rome. The church had been founded in Jerusalem, and the early ecumenical councils were composed of delegates from various churches who met as equals. 588 AD, however, marked the beginning of a great power struggle and rivalry between Rome (West) and Constantinople (East). It was a power struggle that accelerated the Bishop of Rome to take on the title of "Universal Bishop." The papacy began in earnest in the year 590, with Gregory I, as Gregory the Great, who consolidated the power of the bishopric in Rome and started on a new path. He was the first pope who can, with perfect clarity, be given the title of "pope." There is no clear and accurate unbroken succession line of popes from Peter to Gregory I, and certainly the bishops of the Roman Church did not possess the authority over the churches that the pope claims today. Gregory wrote that leadership of the Church had been entrusted by Jesus to Peter, "the prince of all apostles." On Peter's death, Gregory said leadership passed from Peter to

Peter's successors, the bishops of Rome. From Gregory's time onward, the Western Church came to be organized more and more around the papacy as the focal point of authority and leadership.

For Seventy-two Years the Seat of the Papacy Resided in France

In *The Story of the Christian Church*, author William Manchester writes:

> The growth of papal power while upward was not constant. But between 1073 and 1216 AD, about 150 years, the papacy stood in almost absolute power, not only over the church but over the nations of Europe as well. From 1305, for more than seventy years, all the popes were chosen under the orders of the kings of France, and were subservient to their will. From 1305 to 1377 is known as the Babylonish Captivity. At the behest of the French king the seat of the papacy was transferred from Rome to Avignon, in the south of France. The popes became figure- heads under French rule. There were popes and anti-popes in different lands. Papal orders were

> disobeyed freely, excommunications were ignored; for example Edward III of England ordered the papal legate out of his kingdom.

At the urging of Catherine of Siena, Pope Gregory XII returned the papacy from Avignon back to Rome in 1377. In 1414, three popes claimed to be the true successor of Peter, but at the Council of Constance (1414–1418) all three were dethroned, and a new pope, Martin V, was elected as the legitimate pope.

The Renaissance period marked a very low point in the history of the papacy as never before seen heights of corruption and immorality were reached in the Vatican under Roderigo Borgia, who ruled as Pope Alexander VI (1492–1503), and also under Pope Sixtus IV, Pope Innocent VIII, and Pope Leo X, who was a Medici.

No Biblical or Historical Evidence of Peter as Bishop of Rome

The question of whether Peter ever served as Bishop of Rome is one of great debate and interest. Nowhere in the Scripture is this confirmed. In fact, there is very little evidence, if any, that Peter was in Rome, except shortly before his execution and death. In his epistle Peter speaks of Christians in Babylon, and some theologians have interpreted this to mean

Rome. It is indeed odd that Paul would not mention Peter as Bishop of Rome in his correspondence to the Church at Rome. When Paul actually visited Rome, the saints in Rome greeted him, but there was no sign of Peter. Later, when Paul was in prison in Rome writing to the churches in Philippi, Colosse, and Ephesus, he sent greetings from Christians in Rome, but never mentions Peter. As a matter of fact, in his letter to the Colossians there is an extensive list of Christians from Rome, but nowhere on the list can Peter's name be found. Near Paul's death in Rome, only Luke was with him, but there is no mention of Peter. It is also clear from Paul's Epistle to the Galatians Church, Chapters 1 and 2, that Paul did not consider Peter his superior and, at one point, even rebukes Peter.

Paul writing in Galatians 2:7–9, "*On the contrary, recognizing that I had been entrusted with the gospel for the uncircumcised, just as Peter was for the circumcised (for he who worked through Peter as his apostle among the Jews had been at work in me for the gentiles), and recognizing, too, the favor bestowed on me, those who were the acknowledged pillars, James, Cephas, and John, gave Barnabas and me the handclasp of fellowship, signifying that we should go to the Gentiles as they to the Jews.*"

Based on this passage of God's Word, Paul rather than Peter would have been the logical choice to head the Church at Rome. Rome was the capital of the Roman Empire, the center of the Gentile world! Paul (not Peter) was the one chosen to be the apostle to the Gentiles. Still today, more than 99 percent of Catholic Church members are Gentiles, not Jews. We also know that Paul did not consider Peter superior to himself from, 2 Corinthians 12:11, ". . . *Even though I am nothing, I am in no way inferior to the 'super-apostles.'*" But, as it is, the only head of the true church is the Lord Jesus Himself (Ephesians 5:23; Colossians 1:18)!

The Apostle Paul Wrote Thirteen of the Twenty-seven Books of the New Testament

Of the eight known New Testament authors, the apostle Paul was selected by the Holy Spirit to write thirteen of the twenty-seven books of the New Testament (48 percent of the books – 32% of the text), or more books than John (5), Peter (2), Luke (2), Matthew (1), Mark (1), and James (1), combined. This does not include the book of Hebrews, which some scholars also attribute to Paul. Peter's two Epistles account for only 7.4 percent of the New Testament text.

Even though Paul was a Pharisee by training, and as such a logical choice to preach to the Jews, Christ selected him to go to the Gentiles, who would ultimately dominate the Christian faith. Paul's legacy as a preacher of God's Word would eventually include over 30 percent of the world's population, or 2.1 billion people, who today claim to be Christian. Conversely, Peter's lasting legacy as a preacher of the gospel was relatively modest in comparison, as the Jews resisted

Christ as more Gentiles accepted Christ. This would strongly suggest that Paul, not Peter, was the natural leader of the Apostolic Church.

Clearly, Matthew 16:18, 19 is the most critical Scripture for the Catholic Church, as the Church takes its position on "authority" from its interpretation of this particular Scripture. As for Matthew 16:18, 19, non-Catholic theologians favored a much different interpretation than the one settled on by the Catholic Church. They said that the name Peter is from *petros*, a masculine form of the Greek word for "small stone," whereas "rock" is from *petra,* a different form of the same basic word, referring to a rocky mountain or peak. In this verse (18), Jesus was comparing Peter, a small stone, to the great mountainous rock on which He (Christ) would build His church. This rock is referring to Peter's divinely inspired confession of Jesus as "*the Christ, the son of the living God.*" Hence, the rock that the Church is built on is this "faith in Christ," not Peter. Also, in Matt 18:18 Christ bestows all the Matt 16:19 powers on all the apostles.

Christ Alone is the Foundation and Head of His Church

Interestingly, Matthew 16:18–19 aside, the rest of the New Testament makes it abundantly clear that Christ alone is the foundation and head of His church. Acts 4:11, for example, reads, "*This Jesus is 'the stone rejected by you builders which has become the cornerstone.' There is no salvation in anyone else, for there is no other name in the whole world given to men by which we are to be saved.*" In 1 Corinthians 3:11 we read, "*No one can lay a foundation other than the one that has been laid, namely Jesus Christ.*" In 1 Peter 2:6–8, Peter himself describes Jesus as the Chief cornerstone (rock). In 1 Peter 5:4, Peter describes Jesus, not himself, as "The Chief Shepherd," a term that has been associated with popes. In 1 Peter 5:1, Peter calls himself a "fellow elder," not Pope or head of the Church, but simply an elder. Paul writes, "*He* (God) *has put all things under Christ's feet and has made Him, thus exalted, head of the church*" (Eph. 1:22).

It was clear the Lord did not establish His church on the supremacy of Peter; this was made apparent a short while later in the text after Peter's great confession. When the disciples asked Jesus, "*who was greatest in the Kingdom of Heaven?*" He replied by placing a small child before them saying, "*I assure you, unless you change and become like little children, you will not enter the kingdom of God*" (Matthew 18:3).

Had the twelve apostles understood Jesus' teaching about the rock and the keys of the kingdom as referring exclusively to Peter, they would not have asked who was the greatest in the kingdom. Or, had they forgotten or misunderstood Jesus' previous teaching, He would have answered by naming Peter as the greatest and probably would also have chided them for not remembering or believing what He had already taught.

Another example of this is found later in Matthew 20:20–21 when James and John asked Jesus for the top two places of honor in His kingdom, to sit at his right and left. Clearly, they would never have made that request if they had understood that Peter had been given the primacy as Christ's successor. Additional Scriptures that confirm Christ as head of the church are, Eph. 5:23,24, 25 "*. . . As Christ is head of His body the church; . . .*" Psalm 118:22, "*The stone which the builders rejected has become the cornerstone. By the Lord this has been done; it is wonderful in our eyes.*" Colossians 1:18 states, "*It is He who is head of the body, the church.*"

The Apostle Peter Never Claimed a Superior Title over the Other Apostles

It is important to recognize that Peter himself never claimed a superior title, rank, or privilege over the other apostles. He even referred to himself as a "servant and apostle" (1Peter 1:1; 2 Peter 1:1). Far from claiming honor and homage for himself, he soberly warned his fellow elders to guard against lording it over those under their pastoral care, (1 Peter 5:3). It would be hard to imagine that the humble, spiritually-minded, former fisherman, Peter, would be able to identify with the pope in the lush Vatican accommodations (before Pope Francis) with his elaborate triple-decked gold-jeweled miter, who for certain ceremonies, is even carried on the shoulders of bearers, surrounded by the Swiss military guard. A student of history would be hard pressed to find many striking similarities between the Christian Church at the time of the Apostolic Age and what has evolved as the Roman Catholic Church over the last seventeen hundred years.

Peter was the leader of the apostles, but he was also a follower and was at times actually sent by other apostles (Acts 8:12), held accountable for his actions by the Jerusalem church (Acts 11:1–18), and rebuked by Paul (Gal. 2:11–14). Peter was clearly the first of equals among the Apostles but clearly not a supreme authority over the other Apostles or the churches.

Even if Matthew 16:17–18 is interpreted as Peter being the foundation of the church, still the text says nothing about Peter's successors, infallibility, or exclusive authority. The apostles had no successors, for to succeed them one needed to be a witness of Christ's resurrection (see Acts 1:21, 22). Look only five verses ahead in the text to verse 23, where Jesus said to Peter, "*Get behind Me, Satan! You are a stumbling block to Me, you do not have in mind the things of God, but the things of men.*" Here Jesus calls Peter, whom He allegedly had just appointed the infallible "Vicar of Christ" and head of the Church, both Satan and a stumbling block because he denied the necessity of Christ's death and resurrection. This Scripture context does not support Peter as the head of the church.

The church was built on the apostle Peter's confession of faith, *"You are the Christ, the Son of the living God"* (Matthew 16:16). The church is not a building, nor an institution, nor a religious denomination; it is a spiritual gathering of the "called;" an assembly of the justified and the redeemed, who meet to worship the very God who "called them" and justified them. God speaks to those He called and justified through His Word that is preached from the Scriptures in the local assembly of believers, that they might grow spiritually to be more like the Son. By its nature the local assembly also includes unsaved individuals.

The Apostle John Lived Some Thirty Years after the Death of the Apostle Peter

If one is to believe the Catholic Church's teaching on Peter being the first pope, then one would have to believe that Peter's immediate successors as Bishop of Rome (Linus A.D. 64–67, Anacletus I A.D. 76–88, and Clement I A.D. 88–97) all in turn had authority over the Apostle John, who was still alive after Peter's death and wrote the Book of Revelation around A.D. 94–96. It would have been unthinkable that any of the apostles, let alone Christ's favorite apostle, John, would have been under the authority of the three relatively minor individuals that the Catholic Church claims were the first three successors of Peter as Bishop of Rome.

In *The MacArthur Study Bible*, John MacArthur writes:

Although he was greatly advanced in age when he penned First John, John was still actively ministering to the churches. He was the sole remaining apostle survivor who had intimate, eyewitness association with Jesus throughout His earthly ministry, death, resurrection, and ascension. The church Fathers (e.g., Justin Martyr, Irenaeus, Clement of Alexandria, Eusebius) indicate that after that time, John lived in Ephesus in Asia Minor, carrying out an extensive evangelistic program, overseeing many of the churches that had arisen, and conducting an extensive writing ministry. As the last remaining apostle, John's testimony was highly authoritative among the churches. Many eagerly sought to hear the one who had first-hand experience with the Lord Jesus.

The Catholic Church Elects Cardinal Jorge Bergoglio, as the 266th Bishop of Rome

Finally, the election of Argentina's Cardinal Jorge Mario Bergoglio, as the 266th Bishop of Rome by the Catholic Church on March 13, 2013, pledging to clean up the Holy See's scandal-plagued government, is being heralded by many Catholics and non-Catholics alike as a hopeful sign of real reform in the Catholic Church. Less than ninety days after election, Pope Francis established a high-powered committee aimed at reforming the scandal ridden Vatican bank. On June 28, 2013, Monsignor Nunzio Scarano, an official of the Vatican bank, was arrested in connection with a large money-laundering scheme. A leading Catholic Commentator says that Pope Francis has pressed the "reset button" for the Catholic Church.

Pope Francis, on a pilgrimage to the small town of Assisi, said, "This is a good occasion to invite the Church to strip itself of worldliness," said in a room where St. Francis renounced his wealthy family and set out to serve the poor. "There is a danger that threatens everyone in the Church, all of us. The danger of worldliness. It leads us to vanity, arrogance and pride," added the Pope. "A few days after his election, he said he wanted to see 'a church that is poor and for the poor.' He has shunned the spacious papal apartments for Spartan quarters in a Vatican guest house and has urged all clergy, regardless of rank, to get out among the poor and needy" (*Sky News* 10/4/13).

Pope Francis's words in Assisi, follow even stronger words for the church several weeks earlier when he said, "Leaders of the church have often been narcissists, gratified and sickeningly excited by their courtiers . . . I don't share this view, and I will do all I can to change it" (WSJ 10/2/13). While many are hopeful, it remains to be seen what Pope

Francis will be able to achieve in the highly bureaucratic Vatican Curia.

Papal Infallibility—The Catholic Church states, "'The Roman Pontiff, head of the college of bishops, enjoys this infallibility in virtue of his office, when, as supreme pastor and teacher of all the faithful—who confirms his brethren in the faith—he proclaims by a definitive act a doctrine pertaining to faith or morals. . . . The infallibility promised to the Church is also present in the body of bishops when, together with Peter's successor, they exercise the supreme Magisterium,' above all in an Ecumenical Council. When the Church through its supreme Magisterium proposes a doctrine 'for belief as being divinely revealed,' and as the teaching of Christ, the definitions 'must be adhered to with the obedience of faith.' This infallibility extends as far as the deposit of divine Revelation itself" (CCC para. 891).

When we look at the life of the apostle Peter, whom the Roman Catholic Church believes was the first pope, we see that he was not infallible in matters of faith and morals. Paul wrote about Peter's wrong thinking in the Book of Galatians: "*When Cephas* (Peter) *came to Antioch I directly withstood him, because he was clearly in the wrong. He had been taking his meals with the Gentiles before others came who were from James* (Jews). *But when they arrived he drew back to avoid trouble with those who were circumcised. . . . As soon as I observed that they were not being straightforward about the truth of the gospel, I had this to say to Cephas in the presence of all: 'If you are a Jew are living according to Gentile ways rather than Jewish, by what logic do you force the Gentiles to adopt Jewish ways'*" (Galatians 2:11–14). The apostle John writes this about Peter's erroneous thinking: "'*Lord,' Peter said to Him, 'why can I not follow you now? I will lay down my life for You!' 'You will lay down your life for Me, will you?' Jesus answered. 'I tell you the truth, the cock will not crow before you have three times disowned Me*'" (John 13:37–38).

Nothing of this concept of infallibility was known in the early church. Certainly the great theologians such as Irenaeus, who was a disciple of Polycarp, wrote against many heresies of various kinds, but Irenaeus never taught that Christ intended any bishop to be the infallible head of the church. Tertullian was the greatest theologian of the early church before Augustine and never wrote of an infallible head of the church.

Gregory the Great (590 to 604 A.D.) was an ardent defender of the Catholic Church traditions, but Gregory never taught that he was the "infallible head" of the whole church. Even church councils, such as the Council of Constance in 1415 and the Council of Basel in 1432, declared, "even the pope is bound to obey the councils." At another time it was held that infallibility lay in acts of the councils approved by the pope. But it was not until 1870 that infallibility was declared to reside in the pope alone, and all Roman Catholics were compelled to accept that view.

Catholic author Anthony E. Gilles writes:

> The decree on papal infallibility (at the First Vatican Council in 1870) was clearly an innovation in Church doctrine." He goes on to say, "Few Catholic thinkers, even in the Middle Ages, would have gone this far in establishing the pope's authority to proclaim dogma. Further, the decree was made canonically binding on Catholics. In other words, one could not legitimately consider oneself a Catholic unless one accepted the decree on papal infallibility. Again, few theologians would have gone to this extreme in the Middle Ages (*People of God*).

Infallibility Dogma Established by Vote at Vatican Council I

In 1870, at the Vatican I Council on papal infallibility, Pope Pius IX, who was Italian, controlled the Council. Out of the 541 prelates from Europe, 276 represented the Italian peninsula, with a population of only 27 million, or 11 million more than the continent, including Ireland and Britain. The Church historian Philip Schaff said that there was strong opposition to the call for the council, and that delegates representing 80 million Roman Catholics were opposed to it. In spite of this, opposition was futile and could mean reprisals affecting the delegates' present positions or be a detriment to any prospect for future promotion. Before the final vote was taken, 410 bishops petitioned in favor of the dogma pushed by the pope and the very strong Jesuits, and 162 voted against it.

A number of bishops and cardinals opposed papal infallibility. The discussions in the council were cut short as many did not want to be officially on record against it because with a vote against the decree, this anathema would be attached: "If any one—which may God forbid!—shall presume to contradict this our definition, let him be anathema." The final vote on papal infallibility was 533 yes, 2 no, with 106 absent. Those absent and "no" votes had to submit or face excommunication. Most on the council acquiesced to this tradition!

As for the established papacy and hierarchy of authority for the church, Jesus instructed the apostles to avoid ruling the saints in the church in this way. However, today we see within the Catholic Church a huge structure of priests, monsignors, bishops, archbishops, cardinals, and the pope ruling over the parishioners. In the Book of Matthew Jesus tells us what the characteristics of His church leadership should look like. We read the following in Matthew 20:25–26: "*Jesus then called them together and said: 'You know how those who exercise authority among the Gentiles lord it over them; their great ones make their importance felt. It cannot be like that with you. Anyone among you who aspires to greatness must serve the rest, and whoever wants to rank first among you must serve the needs of all.'"*

Popes that spoke in error on matters of faith and morals, when speaking ex-cathedra:

* Pope Liberius (352–366)—Denied the deity of Christ
* Pope Zosimus (417–418)—Denied the necessity of God's grace for salvation
* Pope Vigilius (537–555)—Was condemned as a heretic by a church council
* Pope Honorius (625–638)—Excommunicated for embracing heresy

<u>contradiction of papal decisions:</u>

Pope Sixtus V (1585–1591)—recommended reading the Bible
Pope Pius VII (1800–1823)—condemned reading the Bible
Pope Adrian II (867–872)—declared civil marriages valid
Pope Pius VII (1800–1823)—condemned civil marriages
Pope Martin V (May 1431)—burned Joan of Arc at the stake
Pope Benedict XV (1920)—made Joan of Arc a saint

The Bible Teaches That God Alone Is Infallible

The Bible teaches that God alone is infallible. We read in Numbers 23:19, "*God is not man that He should speak falsely, nor human, that He should change His mind. Is He one to speak and not act, to decree and not fulfill?*" It is also clear from Paul's writing in Acts 17:11, that Scripture itself, not any man, is the only infallible interpreter of Scripture: "*Its members* (Berean Church) *were better disposed than those in Thessalonica, and welcomed the message* (gospel) *with great enthusiasm. Each day they studied the Scriptures to see whether these things were so.*" Further, Paul admonishes the Galatians against distorting the gospel of Christ by adding to it, and effectively going over to another gospel: "*But there is no other. Some who wish to alter the gospel of Christ must have confused you. For even if we, or an angel from heaven, should preach to you a gospel not in accord with the one we delivered to you, let a curse be upon him*" (Galatians 1:7–8).

The Infallibility of the Scriptures is also proven by the Scriptures themselves in the Old Testament, as the Scriptures infallibly interpret themselves:

"*The law of the Lord is perfect, refreshing the soul; The decree of the Lord is trustworthy, giving wisdom to the simple. The precepts of the Lord are right, rejoicing the heart; The command of the Lord is clear, enlightening the eye; The fear of the Lord is pure, enduring forever; The ordinances of the Lord are true, all of them just; They are more precious than gold; than a heap of purest gold; Sweeter also than syrup from the comb*" (Psalm19:8–11).

These passages from the Psalms all refer to God's written Scripture, as God gives His written Word six different titles in these verses: the law, decree, precepts, command, fear, and ordinances. It is clear that these passages are from the Lord as, "of the Lord," is stated six separate times. These passages make it clear that God intended the infallible Scriptures to be His manual for man's worship of God. This left no room for a separate manual for living, created from man-made traditions declared by the popes and the Magisterium of the Catholic Church, which could never measure up to God's perfect manual on faith and morals, the Bible.

Baptism—The *Catechism of the Catholic Church* says, "The Church does not know of any means other than Baptism that assures entry into eternal beatitude; this is why she takes care not to neglect the mission she has received from the Lord to see that all who can be baptized are 'reborn of water and the Spirit.' God has bound salvation to the Sacrament of Baptism . . ." (CCC para.1257).

Additionally, CCC para. 1263 says, "By Baptism all sins are forgiven, original sin and all personal sins, as well as all punishment for sin. In those who have been reborn nothing remains that would impede their entry into the Kingdom of God, neither Adam's sin, nor personal sin, nor the consequences of sin, the gravest of which is separation from God."

One of the Bible verses often used to try to demonstrate that salvation is by baptism is John 3:5, *"I solemnly assure you, no one can enter into God's kingdom without being begotten of water and spirit."* In this verse, however, Jesus is not referring to literal water but to the need for "cleansing." When the word "water" is used figuratively in the Old Testament it usually refers to renewal or spiritual cleansing, especially when used in relationship with "spirit (Psalm 51:9-10; Isaiah 32:15; 44:3-5; 55:1-3; Jeremiah 2:13). Jesus was making reference to the spiritual washing or purification of the soul, accomplished by the Holy Spirit through the Word of God at the moment of salvation (Ephesians 5:26), which was required to belong to His kingdom.

Another verse commonly used in an attempt to show that baptism saves you is found in First Peter and reads, *"You are now saved by a baptismal bath which corresponds to this exactly. This baptism is no removal of physical stain, but the pledge of God of an irreproachable conscience through the resurrection of Jesus Christ"* (1 Peter 3:21). This verse when put in context is Peter teaching that the fact that eight people were in Noah's ark and went through the whole judgment, and yet were unharmed, is analogous to the Christian experience in salvation by being in Christ, the ark of one's salvation. Peter is not at all referring to water baptism here but rather a figurative immersion into union with Christ as an ark of safety from the judgment of God. To be sure he is not misunderstood, Peter clearly says he is not speaking of water baptism in the phrase, *"this baptism is no removal of physical stain."*

What does the Bible say about baptism? The Bible speaks of four distinct types of baptism. John the Baptist baptized with water for repentance. John the Baptist said that one was coming that would baptize with the Holy Spirit and would baptize with fire. Finally, Scripture describes a Christian baptism that was a public sign of a believer's identification with Christ.

John's water baptism—John the Baptist was the last Old Testament prophet and a figure of the prophet Elijah, who is described in 1 and 2 Kings. He baptized as a symbol of repentance for the forgiveness of sins, and he was beheaded before Christ's death on the cross satisfied the penalty for all of man's sin.

The symbolism of John's baptism likely had its origins in purification rituals like those found in the book of Leviticus, Chapter 15, and verse 13. Baptism had a long history in Judaism as Gentile proselytes came into Judaism. The baptism of John dramatically symbolized repentance. Jews accepting John's baptism were admitting they had been as Gentiles and needed to become people of God both inwardly and outwardly. The Jews and Gentiles being baptized were repenting in anticipation of the long awaited Messiah's arrival.

Jesus' baptism by John was the official introduction of Jesus' earthly ministry, and signaled the ending of the Old Covenant and the beginning of the New Covenant, which would provide for the forgiveness of sins through the death of Christ. By Christ's baptism He showed that His ministry was to save sinners. By His baptism He symbolically demonstrated that He would die, be buried, and be raised from the dead. By His baptism Christ showed the power of His ministry, as the Holy Spirit descended on Him as a dove and, God the Father proclaimed in His voice, "*This is my beloved Son, My favor rests on Him*" (Matthew 3:17).

Baptism of the Holy Spirit—John the Baptist foretold of the "Baptism of the Holy Spirit," in (Matthew 3:11), "*I baptize you in water for the sake of reform, but the one who will follow me is more powerful than I . . . He it is who will baptize you in the Holy Spirit. . . .*" Sinners by believing in Christ would receive the "Baptism of the Holy Spirit." In John 7:39, we read, "*He (Jesus) spoke of the Spirit, whom those who believed in Him were to receive. The Spirit, of course, had not yet been given, since Jesus had not yet been glorified.*" In (Romans 8:9) Paul said, "*If anyone does not have the Spirit of Christ, he does not belong to Christ.*" That's what the church was, every believer possessing the Spirit for truth, for instruction, for power, for comfort, for security. The Spirit is in every true believer. The church is born in Acts 2, and from there on every believer at the point of faith in Christ receives the Holy Spirit.

Christ Himself named this event in the believer's life "the baptism of the Holy Spirit." Jesus said in Acts 1:5, "*For John truly baptized with water, but you shall be baptized with the Holy Spirit not many days from now.*" He was talking about what would happen ten days from then, at Pentecost, after His glorification. 1 Corinthians 12:13 reads, "*For by one Spirit*"—that's the same Spirit—"*were we all baptized into one body.*" That's what the baptism of the Spirit does. It takes a person at salvation and places him in the body of Christ. Unlike water baptism, Spirit baptism is not an experience to seek but a reality to acknowledge as Christians.

At salvation, all believers not only become full members of Christ's body, the church, but the Holy Spirit is placed within each of them. We read in (Romans 8:9) "*But you are not in the flesh; you are in the Spirit, since the Spirit of God dwells in you. But if anyone does not have the Spirit of Christ, he does not belong to Christ.*"

Salvation Is by Faith Alone

It is clear from Scripture that salvation is by faith alone, and at the moment that we first accept Christ into our hearts as Lord and Savior, we are indeed baptized by the Holy Spirit with an assurance of eternal salvation. After a confession of faith and the baptism of the Holy Spirit, the new believer is then baptized by water as a public symbol of that original confession of faith. Therefore, the only type of baptism resulting in one's salvation is the Baptism of the Holy Spirit.

We see a complete picture of this truth revealed in Titus 3:5–7 (NAB updated), which reads, "*He saved us, not on the basis of deeds which we have done in righteousness* (like water baptism), *but according to His mercy, by the washing* (divine cleansing) *of regeneration and renewing by the Holy Spirit, whom He poured out upon us richly through Jesus Christ our Savior* (Baptism of the Holy Spirit), *so that being justified by His grace we would be made heirs according to the hope of eternal life*."

In Acts 8:12 we read, "*Once they began to believe in the Good News that Philip preached about the kingdom of God and the name of Jesus Christ* (Baptism of the Holy Spirit), *men and women alike accepted* (water) *baptism*." Faith and Baptism of the Holy Spirit came first, and water baptism second.

If a person repents of their sin, and accepts Jesus Christ as their Lord, Master, and Redeemer; but they die before they can receive water baptism, do they go to heaven? If we say yes, as most Catholics would, then they must be saved by their faith.

Baptism of Fire—In the context used in Matthew 3:11 fire is used throughout verses 10, 11, and 12 as a means of judgment, so we can conclude that this use of fire must speak of a baptism of judgment that Christ will administer on the unrepentant on Judgment Day. We know that this fire has nothing to do with the "tongues that looked like fire" at Pentecost, because we see this "fire" defined in verse 12. "*His winnowing fan is in his hand and he cleared the threshing floor and gathered his grain into the barn, but he will burn up the chaff with unquenchable fire*." This is clearly a picture of the fire of eternal judgment. This verse, Matthew 3:11, is saying that you are either baptized with the Holy Spirit unto salvation or in the end you are baptized with the fire of eternal judgment and damnation.

Christian Baptism—The first Christian baptism is described in Acts 2:38. Christian baptism differed from John's baptism in that it altered the significance of the ritual, symbolizing publicly the believer's identification with Christ in His death, burial, and resurrection. When the believer is submerged in water, it symbolizes His death and burial with Christ, and when the believer is raised out of the water, it symbolizes his resurrection with Christ. Christian baptism was commanded by Christ in the Great Commission, which we can read in (Matthew 28:19) when Christ says, "*Go therefore and make disciples of all nations, baptizing them in the name of the Father and the Son and the Holy Spirit*." A Christian baptism is administered in the name of the Father, the Son, and the Holy Spirit, which was not part of John's Old Testament baptism.

That Christian baptism does not save us from our sins is clearly shown in Acts 10:43-47, which reads, "*To Him all the prophets testify that everyone who believes in Him has forgiveness of sins through His name*." Note that it does not say that forgiveness is through baptism, but rather through believing in His name. "*Peter had not finished these words when the Holy Spirit descended upon all who were listening to Peter's message*." ". . .*What can stop these people who have received the Holy Spirit from being baptized with water?*" Salvation came first and water baptism second.

The distinct difference between John's baptism and Christian baptism can be shown in Acts 19:1–7, as Paul found some disciples in Ephesus and asked, "'*Did you receive the Holy Spirit when you became believers?' They answered, 'we have not so much as heard that there is a Holy Spirit.' 'Well, how were you baptized? He persisted.' They replied,* 'with the baptism of John.' *Paul then explained, 'John's baptism was a baptism of repentance. He use to tell the people to believe in Him who was coming after him, that is, in Jesus.' When they heard this they were baptized again, but this time in the name of the Lord Jesus*.'"

The disciples of John the Baptist whom Paul found in Ephesus were Old Testament seekers. They did not fully understand the Christian faith. Since all Christians receive the Holy Spirit at the moment of salvation (Romans 8:9; 1 Cor. 12:13), their confused and uncertain answers told Paul that these disciples of John the Baptist were not yet truly Christians, so Paul gave them instructions, not on how to receive the Holy Spirit, but about Jesus Christ. They believed Paul's presentation of the gospel and came to saving faith in the Lord Jesus Christ, receiving the Holy Spirit, but only then did they receive Christian baptism.

As he does in Romans 4:3, Paul again uses Galatians 3:6–9 as proof that there has never been any other way of salvation than by grace through faith. In the following passages Paul uses the Old Testament and quotes Genesis 15:6 to show that believing Jews and Gentiles are true spiritual children of Abraham because they follow his example of faith, apart from baptism or any other good deed: "*Consider the case of Abraham: he 'believed God, and it was credited to him as justice.' This means that those who believe are sons of Abraham. Because Scripture saw in advance that God's way of justifying the Gentiles would be through faith, it foretold this good news to Abraham: 'All nations shall be blessed in you.' Thus it is that all who believe are blessed along with Abraham, the man of faith*" (Gal. 3:6–9).

Infant baptism—The Catholic Catechism says, "Born with a fallen human nature and tainted by original sin, children also have need of the new birth in Baptism to be free from the power of darkness and brought into the realm of the freedom of the children of God, to which all men are called. The sheer gratuitousness of the grace of salvation is particularly manifest in infant Baptism. The Church and the parents would deny a child the priceless grace of becoming a child of God were they not to confer Baptism shortly after birth" (CCC para. 1250).

"As regards children who have died without Baptism, the Church can only entrust them to the mercy of God" (CCC para. 1261). The *Trent Catechism* is even more specific saying, "Infants unless regenerated unto God through the grace of baptism, whether their parents be Christian or infidel, are born to eternal misery and perdition."

Limbo Doctrine Abandoned by the Roman Catholic Church

This Catholic doctrine, from the Council of Trent, was so unthinkable and unacceptable to the laity that it was found necessary to invent a third realm, the *Limbus Infantum* (Limbo), to which unbaptized infants are sent and are excluded from heaven but suffer no positive pain. It is interesting to note that Limbo, has now fallen out of favor, and Pope Benedict XVI abandoned this long-held concept.

The Roman Catholic Church has now effectively buried the concept of Limbo, with its April, 2007 authorized publication of the 41-page document, called *The Hope of Salvation for Infants who die without being Baptized*."

Infant baptism did not appear in the church until the second and third centuries as the hierarchy of the Church began to evolve. In the Apostolic Church, a confession of faith was necessary before baptism by water. It would have been impossible, therefore, for an infant to make this confession of faith. Baptism by water was a public symbol of one's previous confession of faith but had no saving value in itself. A profession of faith came first, and baptism followed.

One of the key passages often used by Catholic apologists in an attempt to confirm infant baptism biblically is the following verses from the Book of Acts, after Paul and Silas were released from prison in Philippi and assisted by the Philippian jailer, who wanted to be saved: '"*...Men, what must I do to be saved?' Their answer was, 'Believe in the Lord Jesus and you will be saved, and all your household.' They proceeded to announce the word of God to him and to everyone in his house. At that late hour of the night he took them in and bathed their wounds; then he and his whole household were baptized'*" (Acts 16:30-33). The Catholic assumption is that the "whole household" by definition must include some infants.

First, "whole household" would include the jailer's family, servants, and guests. Second, it is clear from the passage that salvation must come from believing in the Lord. Paul says, "*Believe in the Lord and you will be saved.*" No where does it say or even imply that salvation is through baptism. In order to believe in the Lord the members of the household had to hear and comprehend the gospel message (they proceeded to announce the word of God to them), and then have the intellectual capacity to believe, which is faith. This clearly could not include infants, who would not be able to understand the gospel message or understand it. If indeed there were infants in the household, the better assumption is that they were all asleep, since it was late at night. No where in the pages of Scripture do we see infants being baptized.

Baptism by sprinkling water—The practice of sprinkling water to baptize rather than full emersion began after the Apostolic Age. The first specifically documented case of sprinkling involved a man by the name of Novatian (ca. A.D. 250), who lived in Rome. Novatian was believed to be at the point of death and so was sprinkled in his sick bed. However, the case was very unusual.

Eusebius of Caesarea (ca. A.D. 263–339), known as the father of church history, described the incident. He wrote that Novatian thereafter was restricted from being appointed as a church officer. Why was this? Because it was not deemed "lawful" that one administered "baptism" by "aspersion" (sprinkling/pouring), as he was, should be promoted to the order of the clergy" (Ecclesiastical History, VI.XLIII).

Sprinkling for baptism grew during the time of Constantine (circa–A.D. 320), as vast numbers of pagans converted to Christianity to get the advantages of belonging to the newly approved religion of the Holy Roman Empire.

Baptism Is Symbolic of the Death, Burial, and Resurrection of Christ

The Synod of Cologne (A.D.1280) said, "He who baptizes, when he immerses the candidate in water, shall neither add to the words, or take away from them, or change them." It was not until the Council of Ravenna (A.D. 1311) that sprinkling or pouring was made an option for administering baptism by the Catholic Church (Schaff, p.201).

Never do we find a single case in the New Testament of water being brought to a person who was going to be baptized. We read in Acts 8:38, " . . . *and Philip went down into the water with the eunuch and baptized him*." It is necessary for immersion that both the one to be baptized and the one doing the baptizing go down into the water. This would not be necessary in the case of sprinkling or pouring.

Romans 6:4 reads, "*Through baptism into His death we were buried with Him . . .*" Colossians 2:12 reads, "*In baptism you were not only buried with Him but also raised to life with Him . . .*" Baptism as described in these two verses was a burial. When something is buried it is completely covered or submerged. Only immersion can fit the description of a burial. One is not buried in baptism when water is sprinkled or poured over his head.

The theological connection between "baptism" and the burial and resurrection of Christ (Romans 6:3–4; Col. 2:12) negates the notion that the rite may be performed by sprinkling or pouring, which is the tradition in the Roman Catholic Church.

Finally, the Bible says, "*Christ died for sins once for all*" (Hebrews 7:27). "*For by one offering He has perfected for all time [past, present, and future] those who are sanctified*" (Hebrews 10:14). All sin is "all sin," and all time is "all time," and nowhere in Scripture does it say that Christ died only for past sin or only for "original sin." As for children, Christ said, "*. . . I assure you, unless you change and become like little children, you will not enter the Kingdom of God. Whoever makes himself lowly, becoming like this child, is of greatest importance in the heavenly reign*" (Matthew 18:1–4). It is unimaginable that "this Christ" would send an innocent child who dies, anywhere but to Heaven.

Indulgences—The Catechism of the Catholic Church says:

> An indulgence is a remission before God of the temporal punishment due to sins whose guilt has already been forgiven, which the faithful Christian who is duly disposed gains

> under certain prescribed conditions through the action of the Church which, as the minister of redemption, dispenses and applies with authority the treasury of the satisfactions of Christ and the saints. An indulgence is partial or plenary accordingly as it removes either part or all of the temporal punishment due to sin. The faithful can gain indulgences for themselves or apply them to the dead (CCC para. 1471).

Historically, it was in 1096, at the Synod of Clermont, that Pope Urban II promised a plenary indulgence for all who would take part in the Crusades. From this time on, indulgences became a fixed and remunerative part of Catholicism. "Indulgences are part of the Catholic Church's infallible teaching. This means that no Catholic is at liberty to disbelieve in them. The Council of Trent stated that it 'condemns with anathema those who say that indulgences are useless or that the Church does not have the power to grant them' (Trent, Session 25, Decree on Indulgences). Trent's anathema places indulgences in the realm of infallibly defined teaching" (Catholic Answers—Primer on Indulgences).

In *People of God,* author Gilles describes the building project that was the proverbial "straw-that-broke-the-camel's-back" as far as Martin Luther was concerned. That was the building of St. Peter's Basilica. Pope Leo X (1513–1521) had devised a scheme, according to Gilles, to finish St. Peter's Basilica during his pontificate so that his family, the Medicis, would get most of the credit for the project:

> He (Leo X) turned north to wealthy Germany. The prince-elector of Mainz, an archbishop, Albert of Brandenburg, was himself a poor steward of money. He was in arrears on his financial obligations to Rome. Leo proposed a deal. He would authorize a campaign in Albert's diocese to grant plenary indulgences. For purchasing indulgencies, Catholics would be promised in a papal document that all their sins would be forgiven and all time in purgatory for those sins remitted. Albert could keep half of the money he collected, and the pope would get the other half. Albert's back taxes would be wiped out, and Leo would raise money to continue building St. Peter's.

Gilles, describes a Dominican friar named Johan Tetzel, who sold indulgences near the borders of Luther's home near Saxony. Apparently, Tetzel, in his zeal to raise as much money as he could, told parishioners that not only could they save their own souls from purgatory, but with a purchased indulgence they could also free the souls of family and friends that were already in purgatory. Tetzel's companions even sang a little ballad: "*As soon as the coin in the coffer rings, the soul from purgatory to heaven springs.*'"

Indulgences Create a Culture of Corruption in the Church

The corruption connected with the granting or sale of indulgences became so flagrant that clear-thinking men in the clergy and laity alike came to despise the practice. In 1250, Grosseteste, Bishop of Lincoln, England, protested to the pope that the low morality of the priesthood was due to the "purchasable pardon." A commission of cardinals reported to Pope Paul III (1534–1549) that pardons and dispensations produced indescribable scandals and begged him to put an end to them.

The underlying assumption of the Catholic Church with regard to indulgences is that Christ's death is not sufficient for the forgiveness of sins. In addition to the sufferings of Christ, the penitent or some other sinner must also suffer punishment if the penitent will be saved. The Scriptures, however, clearly teach that Christ's death is sufficient payment for sin: "*that justice of God which works through faith in Jesus Christ for all who believe. All men have sinned and are deprived of the glory of God. All men are now undeservedly justified by the gift of God, through the redemption wrought in Christ Jesus. Through His blood, God made Him the means of expiation for all who believe*" (Romans 3:22–25).

Indulgences are clearly in opposition to the Scriptures and are a manmade tradition of the Roman Catholic Church. Historically, they were an enormous source of revenue to the Vatican. Papal indulgencies are not sold today, but they are still granted. It is understood, however, that the faithful who come seeking them do not come empty-handed. The Bible tells us, "*Yet in no way can a man redeem himself, or pay his own ransom to God*" (Psalm 49:8).

Confession—According to the Catholic Church, "Christ instituted the sacrament of Penance for all sinful members of his Church: above all for those who, since Baptism, have fallen into grave sin, and have thus lost their baptismal grace and wounded ecclesial communion. It is to them that the sacrament of Penance offers a new possibility to convert and to recover the grace of justification. The Fathers of the Church present this sacrament as 'the second plank [of salvation] after the shipwreck which is the loss of grace'" (CCC para. 1446).

The Q & A Catholic Catechism by J. A. Hardon, S.J. defines confession: "Penance (confession) is the sacrament instituted by Christ in which sinners are reconciled with God through the absolution (remission) of the priest" (p 263).

Confession was first introduced into the Catholic Church on a voluntary basis in the fifth century by the authority of Leo the Great. But it was not until the Fourth Lateran Council, in 1215, under Pope Innocent III, that private auricular (spoken into the ear) confession was made compulsory, and all Roman Catholic people were required to confess and to seek absolution from a priest at least once a year. The Catholic Church primarily uses Matthew 16:19 to justify confession: "*I will entrust to you the keys of the Kingdom of Heaven; and whatever you declare bound on earth shall be bound in Heaven, and whatever you declare loosed on earth shall be loosed in Heaven.*"

This Catholic doctrine of confession or the "Sacrament of Penance" is also stated in (CCC para. 553): "Jesus entrusted a specific authority to Peter: 'I will give you the keys of the kingdom of heaven, and whatever you bind on earth shall be bound in heaven, and whatever you loose on earth shall be loosed in heaven.' The 'power of the keys' designates authority to govern the house of God, which is the Church. Jesus, the Good Shepherd confirmed this mandate after his Resurrection: 'Feed my sheep.' The power to 'bind and loose' connotes the authority to absolve sin..."

Matthew 16:19, however, represents authority, and here Christ gives Peter (and by extension all other believers) authority to declare what was bound or loosed in heaven. We see this same authority given in John 20:23, where Christ gives all the disciples authority to forgive or retain the sins of the people. This must all be understood in the context of Matthew 18:15-17, where Christ laid out specific instructions for dealing with sin in the church. For example in verse fifteen we read, *"If you brother should commit some wrong* (sin) *against you, go and point out his fault, but keep it between the two of you. If he listens to you, you have won your brother over."*

This means that any duly constituted body of believers, acting in accord with God's Word in the Bible, has the authority to declare if someone is forgiven or un-forgiven. The church's authority is not to determine these things, as only God can do that, but to declare the judgment of heaven based on the principles of Scripture. When they make such a judgment on the basis of God's Word, they can be sure that heaven is in accord. In other words, whatever they "bind" or "loose" on earth is already "bound" or "loosed" in heaven. When the church acknowledges that a repentant person has been loosed from that sin, the church is saying what God says about that person.

We see this truth in Scripture as it relates to the authority given to the apostles to preach the Gospel that contains God's conditions for repentance and forgiveness. "*Penance for the remission of sins*" *was to be* "*preached in His name unto all the nations*" (Luke 24:47). "*To Him all the prophets testify, saying that everyone who believes in Him has forgiveness of sins through His name*" (Acts 10:43). And again, "*You must realize, my brothers, that it is through Him that the forgiveness of sins is being proclaimed to you, including the remission of all those charges you could never be acquitted of under the Law of Moses. In Him, every believer is acquitted*" (Acts 13:38–39). Further scriptural proof that Christ did not intend to have a priest, or anyone acting as an interceder with men is found in 1 Tim 2:5, "*God is One, One also is the mediator between God and men, the man Christ Jesus*." Also, "*Who can forgive sins except God alone*" (Mark 2:7 and Luke 5:21)? This clearly leaves no room for a member of the priesthood hearing man's sins and forgiving them.

Since neither Peter, the apostles, nor their disciples, or the early church fathers practiced going to confession to a priest for absolution of their sins, it is clear that neither Peter or the apostles believed that they had been instructed by Christ to absolve people of their sins as is claimed in (CCC para. 553). It was only in the fifth century that Eastern monastics began the practice of confessing sins to a priest for absolution, and it wasn't until the seventh century that this practice spread to the entire Catholic Church. We know from the Book of Acts that the apostles followed Christ's instructions very closely, but not one instance of confession to anyone for absolution is mentioned. In 2007, just 26 percent of American Catholics said they went to confession at least once a year, down from 74 percent in the early 1980s. (Georgetown University)

Mortal Sin Necessitates a Vehicle of Redemption

The concept of *mortal sin* in the Catholic faith, with its eternal consequences, practically necessitates a vehicle of redemption such as the Sacrament of Penance (confession), to restore the lost Catholic sinner to their former state of grace and salvation.

The Catechism of the Catholic Church defines a mortal sin as, "A grave infraction of the law of God that destroys the divine life in the soul of the sinner (sanctifying grace) constituting a turn away from God. For a sin to be mortal, three conditions must be present: grave matter, full knowledge of the evil act, and full consent of the will" (CCC para. 1855 & 1857). All other sin is considered by the Catholic Church as "venial sin" (meaning "forgivable" sin, or sin not unto death).

The *Catholic View* says that "the concept of mortal sin comes from the First Letter of John, Chapter 5, Verses 16 and 17 in the New Testament: *'If anyone sees his brother sinning, if the sin is not deadly* (venial), *he should pray to God and He will give him life. This is only for those whose sin is not deadly. There is such a thing as deadly sin* (mortal) *about which I do not say that you should pray. All wrong doing is sin, but there is sin that is not deadly* (venial).'"

The MacArthur New Testament Commentary, clarifies this passage in the following manner:

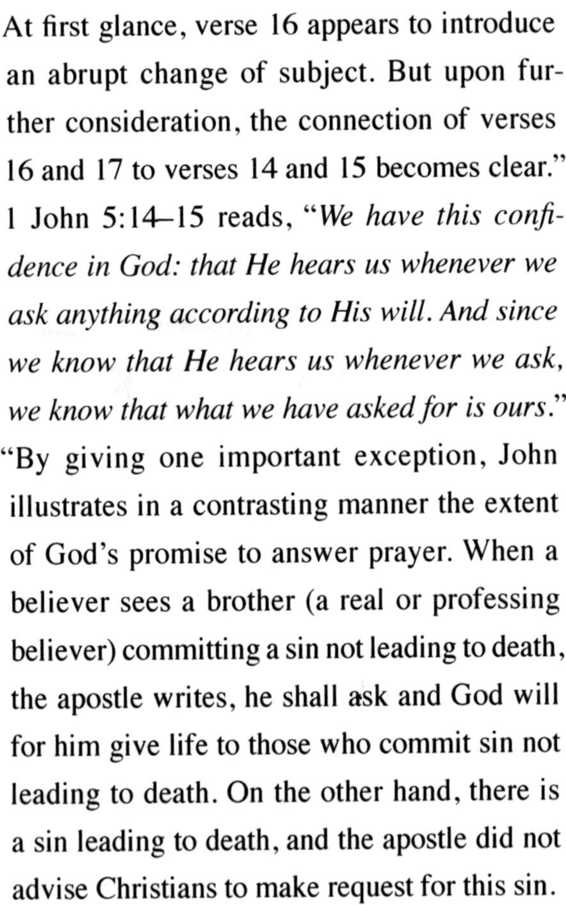

At first glance, verse 16 appears to introduce an abrupt change of subject. But upon further consideration, the connection of verses 16 and 17 to verses 14 and 15 becomes clear." 1 John 5:14–15 reads, "*We have this confidence in God: that He hears us whenever we ask anything according to His will. And since we know that He hears us whenever we ask, we know that what we have asked for is ours*." "By giving one important exception, John illustrates in a contrasting manner the extent of God's promise to answer prayer. When a believer sees a brother (a real or professing believer) committing a sin not leading to death, the apostle writes, he shall ask and God will for him give life to those who commit sin not leading to death. On the other hand, there is a sin leading to death, and the apostle did not advise Christians to make request for this sin.

Blasphemy against the Holy Spirit Is the Only Unforgivable Sin

Further in the Commentary, "Two possibilities present themselves. First, the sin in question may be that of a non-Christian leading to eternal death. In that case it would be a final rejection of Jesus Christ, such as that committed by those who attributed His miracles to the power of Satan (Matt. 12:31–32)." We know from these verses that such ultimate apostasy is unforgivable.

The MacArthur New Testament Commentary continues:

> Another possibility is that John is not referring to an unbeliever, but to a believer. According to this view, the sin leading to death refers to a Christian's sin that is so serious that God takes the life of the one committing it. He put to death Ananias and Sapphira when they lied to the Holy Spirit in front of the church (Acts 5:1–11). We know that Ananias and Sapphira were true believers because they were included in the 'congregation of those who believed,' in (Acts 4:32). They were also involved with the Holy Spirit, thus indicating a relationship with Him. Earthly death can be a divine chastening for a believer, see

(1 Cor. 11:30–32). In this case the sin is not one particular sin, but any sin that the Lord determines is serious enough to warrant such severe chastisement. Although God mercifully does not immediately punish every sin with death, every sin is nonetheless a serious matter to Him.

In the second possibility, that of the true believer, we can have confidence that the death of the sinning brother in 1 John 5:16, was a physical earthly death and not an eternal spiritual death. Many Scripture verses testify to the ultimate security of the true believer, even when he sins, which all believers do.

In a 2012 newspaper column entitled, *My Answer,* Billy Graham wrote, "When we come by faith to Christ and commit our lives to Him, He forgives us all our sins and comes to live within us by His Holy Spirit. He adopts us as His children—and nothing can ever change that. As the Bible says, '*nothing will be able to separate us from the love of God that is in Jesus Christ our Lord*'" (Romans 8:39).

Many other verses in Scripture confirm and support Romans 8:39, showing the absolute security of the true believer. Once he has been saved he cannot then be lost.

Consider the following verses on the security of the believer, from *The New American Catholic Bible:*

Romans 8:35–39 : "*Who will separate us from the love of Christ? Trial, or distress, or persecution, or hunger, or nakedness, or danger, or the sword? . . .For I am certain that neither death nor life, neither angels nor principalities, neither the present nor the future, nor powers, neither height nor depth nor any other creature, will be able to separate us from the love of God that comes to us in Christ Jesus, our Lord.*

John 10:26–*30* : "*My sheep hear My voice. I know them and they follow Me. I give them eternal life and they shall never perish. No one shall snatch them out of My hand. My Father is greater than all, in what He has given Me, and there is no snatching out of His hand. The Father and I are one.*"

John 6:39–40 : "*It is the will of Him who sent Me that I should lose nothing of what He has given Me; rather, that I should raise it up on the last day. Indeed, this is the will of My Father, that everyone who looks upon the Son and believes in Him shall have eternal life. Him I will raise up on the last day.*"

Romans 8:1–2 : "*There is no condemnation now for those who are in Christ Jesus. The law of the spirit, the spirit of life in Christ Jesus, has freed you from the law of sin and death.*"

Ephesians 1:4–5 : "*God chose us in Him before the world began, to be holy and blameless in His sight, to be full of love; he likewise predestined us through Christ Jesus to be His adopted sons—such was His will and pleasure*."

John 11:26 : " . . . *Whoever believes in Me, though he should die, will come to life; and whoever is alive and believes in Me will never die*."

Philippians 1:6 : "*I am sure of this much; that He who has begun the good work in you will carry it through to completion, right up to the day of Christ Jesus*."

John 3:18 : "*Whoever believes in Him avoids condemnation, but whoever does not believe is already condemned for not believing in the name of God's only Son*."

John 5:24 "*I solemnly assure you, the man who hears My Word and has faith in Him who sent Me possesses eternal life. He does not come under condemnation, but has passed from death to life*."

Salvation Is a Free Gift

The above passages confirm and testify to the truth that salvation is a free gift from God that only requires our belief. We find no qualifications for salvation attached to these verses, other than we must believe in Jesus Christ. These passages from Scripture confirm that a person who repents of their sin and believes in Christ and His Gospel can never again be lost but has the security of eternal life. King David and the apostle Paul were great sinners, but they also became two of God's greatest saints.

When Christ died on the cross at Calvary, His once-for-all sacrifice was completed, and the veil of the temple that separated the Holy of Holies (where God was present) from the rest of the temple was torn in two from top to bottom by God's miraculous act. The barrier of sin (the veil) was forever removed for those who put their trust in the Son as Lord and Savior. By coming to the Son, any man could now come to God directly, without the need of priest, sacrifice, or ritual. A believer (the elect) could now confess their sins directly to their only mediator with the Father, Jesus Christ (1 Tim. 2:5), and their sins are forgiven and their relationship with the Father is fully restored, but importantly their ultimate salvation was never in doubt.

If God so loved us that He sacrificed the life of His only begotten Son, when we were still sinners, will He then now fail to give us much less—now that we are sons of God—to keep us saved? Would Christ now condemn us after He died a horrible death on a cross to save us? The only logical answer to these questions is a resounding, NO! Our salvation is based on God's love for us, not our love for Him.

The Catholic Church teaches that a believer can lose their salvation over and over again through mortal sins but can be redeemed over and over again by going to confession and receiving forgiveness and absolution from a Catholic priest, in a process of continuous conversion. The Bible describes only one unforgivable sin, and that is the blasphemy of the Holy Spirit, or rejecting God outright, (Matthew 12:31–32). The Bible teaches that Christ died on Calvary and paid the full price for all of man's sins, past, present, and future (Hebrews 10:11–15), and that the believer is secure in Christ's righteousness, through no merit of their own.

Someone might come along and say, what about a person that made a profession of faith, went to church every Sunday, and lived a moral life for many years. Then suddenly, this person totally rejects God and the Gospel, falls into a life of sin, and will not repent. Is this person still saved? We can read the answer to this question in 1 John 2:19, "*It was from our ranks that they took their leave—not that they really belonged to us; for if they had belonged to us, they would have stayed with us. It only served to show that none of them was ours.*" Those genuinely born again endure in faith and fellowship and truth. The ultimate test of true Christianity is endurance, (Mark 3:13). The departure of people from the truth and the church shows that they were never saved to begin with.

Confession, like many Catholic practices, often mix biblical truth with human tradition, which can be confusing even to Catholics. For example, the centuries-old Catholic tradition of fasting from meat on Fridays as an act of penance, with few exceptions, carried the penalty of mortal sin, if violated. This changed after Vatican II (1962–65), when the Catholic Church in the United States made eating meat on Friday an option, allowing Catholics to choose their own penance instead. This change raised questions among Catholics about the disposition of souls that were apparently "lost in hell" prior to 1966, because they had disobeyed the Church rule and ate meat on a Friday, but they unfortunately died before they could get to a priest to confess this sin and receive absolution. Were these souls still in hell, or were they now in heaven?

In his book, *Preparing for Eternity,* Mike Gendron sums up the eight-step biblical process whereby sinful man is saved from the eternal punishment due for his sin, by the one mediator provided by God, Jesus Christ:

"Sinners are saved . . .

- **from** God's just punishment (2 Thessalonians 1:8–9)
- **by** God's grace, not of works (Ephesians 2:8–9)
- **through** faith in Jesus (John 3:36)
- **because** of God's love and mercy (Titus 3:5; Romans 5:8)
- **only** on the basis of Christ's death and resurrection (1 Corinthians 15:1–4)
- **at** the moment we are born of God (John 1:13)

* **for** God's glory (Ephesians 2:7)
* **throughout** all eternity (Hebrews 5:9; Revelation 22:3–5)"

The issue of confession is not so much about confessing sins to a priest, but about how God's forgiveness of sin is attained. Is forgiveness about God's free gift of grace, or about works of satisfaction? The issue centers on the penance given to the sinner by the priest for satisfaction of his/her confessed sin. Performing or doing works of merit (prayers, rosary, or tasks) to satisfy as contrition for sins violates the above passages on God's free gift, especially Ephesians 2:8–9, "*I repeat, it is owing to His favor that salvation is yours through faith. This is not your own doing, it is God's gift.*"

In Summary, we find no mention of auricular confession in the first century church. No word is found in the writings of the early church fathers regarding the confession of sins to a priest or anyone else seeking absolution, except to God Himself. Tertullian (circa 220), Origen (250), Athanasius (370), Chrysostom (400), Jerome (420), and Nestorius (430) all apparently lived without going to private confession to a priest for absolution.

Confession in the early church was a public matter that related to grave sin and could be done only once. There was no absolution by a priest. Private confession to a priest did not come into prominence until the seventh century and it completely displaced public confession. The assertion by the

Council of Trent (1546) that it was making "binding on all believers" a universal practice of the sacrament of penance that existed from the very beginning, was simply not true. The new Catechism of the Catholic Church (1994) appears to correct Trent and reads, "During the first centuries the reconciliation of Christians who had committed particular grave sins after their baptism was tied to a very rigorous discipline, according to which penitents had to do public penance for their sins for years, before receiving reconciliation...one was rarely admitted and in certain regions only once in a lifetime. During the seventh century Irish missionaries, inspired by the Eastern monastic tradition, took to continental Europe the "private" practice of penance, which does not require public and prolonged completion of penitential works before reconciliation and so opened the way to a regular frequenting of this sacrament. It allowed the forgiveness of grave sins and venial sins to be integrated into one sacramental celebration. In its main lines this is the form of penance that the Church has practiced down to this day" (CCC para. 1447).

Purgatory—*The Catechism of the Catholic Church* defines Purgatory as, "All who die in God's grace and friendship, but still imperfectly purified, are indeed assured of their eternal salvation; but after death they undergo purification, so as to achieve the holiness necessary to enter the joy of heaven" (CCC para. 1030). The Catholic Church formulated her doctrine of purgatory at the Councils of Florence (1439) and

Trent (1545). The original concept of purgatory, however, dates back to Augustine (died A.D.430) who expressed doubt about some aspects of it.

The Catholic Church teaches that even though a sin has been forgiven, punishment must still be paid. This temporal punishment can be paid through acts of penance in this life, such as saying the rosary, a given number of "Hail Mary's" or Our Fathers, or doing good deeds; or it can be paid off in the next life in purgatory, or a combination of both. The living may also help the dead loved one who is in purgatory by gaining credits called indulgences that cancel temporal punishment. Purgatory is described as a place of "cleaning fire." See (CCC para. 1030–1032, 1471–1473).

Belief in purgatory's existence is expressed at every Mass said. During the celebration of the Mass, prayers are offered for the dead. Typically the Mass itself is also offered specifically for someone thought to be suffering in purgatory, usually requested by a family member, who makes a small donation to the priest saying the mass.

Eternal Life is the Unmerited Gift of God

The Bible tell us, however, that eternal life is not a reward for prayers offered or good deeds done, but rather the unmerited gift of God. "*The wages of sin is death, but the gift of God is eternal life in Christ Jesus our Lord*" (Romans 6:23).

The Bible tells us that "*Jesus freed us from our sins by His own blood*" (Revelation 1:5). Scripture makes no mention of acts of indulgences or penance, nor does it describe a place like purgatory where the penalty of sin can be satisfied. If a sinner must pay an additional punishment for his sins, that is the same as saying that Jesus' blood was not sufficient to pay the full price for man's sin. "*But if we acknowledge our sins, He who is just can be trusted to forgive our sins and cleanse us from every wrong*" (1 John 1:9). Jesus paid it all: He Himself is the full atonement for all our sins.

Gilles comments, "To this day, conceptions of hell and purgatory are based largely on medieval imagination rather than on anything found in revelation or official Church doctrine." In Martin Luther's day the offering of Masses and prayers for departed family and friends was very popular in the Catholic Church; the idea was that these Masses and prayers would be credited toward freeing those souls from the purifying fires of purgatory. At times devious priests would be able to gain an even larger "donation" by exaggerating the pain and suffering, even above what they thought the soul might experience.

The primary scriptural justification for purgatory used by the Catholic Church is Matthew 12:32, 1 Corinthians 3:15, and 2 Maccabees 12:44–46. In Matthew 12:32, Jesus warns His detractors of the fact that anyone who commits blasphemy against the Holy Spirit, "*will not be forgiven, either in this age or in the age to come*." Jesus does not say that "some sins" will be forgiven after death, as some have wrongly inferred from His words. Rather, He emphatically declares that he who commits this sin shall never be forgiven. It is erroneous reasoning to say that something will happen in the age to come, only because it is stated that something will not happen in the age to come.

In 1 Corinthians 3:15 the Bible speaks not of redemption in purgatory, but rather of reward in heaven. It speaks not of the destiny of our souls, but of the quality of our work for Jesus Christ. The works in question have nothing to do with our acceptance before God (see Eph. 2:8–9; Titus 3:4–5; and Romans 4:4–5). The text in 2 Maccabees 12:44 reads, "For if he were not expecting the fallen to rise again, it would have been useless and foolish to pray for them in death. But if he did this with a view to the splendid reward that awaits those who had gone to rest in godliness, it was a holy and pious thought. Thus He made atonement for the dead that they might be freed from this sin."

It should be noted that 2 Maccabees is even difficult to reconcile with Roman Catholic teaching because it advocates that soldiers who had died in the mortal sin of idolatry (which cannot be forgiven in Catholic doctrine) should have prayers and sacrifices offered for them with the possibility that they will be delivered from their suffering.

Purgatory: A Tradition of Roman Catholicism

Second, there is no record that Christ or any of the apostles ever quoted from Maccabees or any of the 14 or 15 books of the Apocrypha or that they made any reference to them, although they undoubtedly knew of them. Interestingly, Josephus, the noted Jewish historian, about A.D. 90 gave a list of the books of Jewish law and prophets, but he did not include the Apocryphal books. Other Jewish sources support Josephus. The Apocrypha was rejected by Origen who is generally acknowledged to have been the most learned man in the church before Augustine, by Tertullian, an outstanding scholar in the third century, by Athanasius, the champion of orthodoxy at the Council of Nicaea, and by Jerome, the translator of the *Latin Vulgate,* which became the authorized Roman Catholic Bible. Jerome declared emphatically that the Apocrypha was not part of the Old Testament Scriptures. These books were never regarded as divinely inspired as they did not meet the criteria for canonicity. In spite of this denouncement, fifty-three bishops at the Council of Trent in 1546 pronounced the Apocryphal books canonical and deserving "equal veneration" with the books of the Bible, this almost 2,000 years after the Old Testament was completed and closed. Roman Catholics sometimes charge Protestants with having "cut those books out of the Bible." But the record makes it clear that if anyone excluded them, it was Christ Himself.

One of the best candidates for purgatory in the Bible would have been the thief on the cross who mocked and shouted insults at Christ even as Christ was being crucified. This thief a short time later repented in his plea to Christ for mercy. The fact that this robber was being crucified would indicate that he was more than just a common thief, but was likely also guilty of other greater crimes such as plundering as he was stealing. After his repentance, Christ could have assigned this sinner to purgatory to "undergo purification so he could achieve the holiness necessary to enter the joy of heaven." But Luke 23:43 tells us that Christ spoke these words to the thief that repented: "*I assure you: this day you will be with me in paradise*." This would have been the perfect opportunity for Christ to establish a doctrine such as purgatory, but He did not.

Some have tried to define "paradise," as used in Luke 23:43 as purgatory, but that definition would not even qualify in Catholic doctrine, because the Catholic Church teaches that purgatory is a place to go for purification of imperfections, before joining Christ in heaven. Christ, however, tells the thief on the cross that he will be with "Him" in paradise "on that very day." Paradise was the heavenly abode of the Old Testament saints prior to Christ's Resurrection.

The parable of the laborer is also confirmed in the above scene at the crucifixion. In the parable of the laborer (Matthew 20:1–16; Mark 10:31), the Master (Christ) gave the laborer who spent only an hour in the vineyard the same reward as the laborer who had worked twelve hours. God's economy rewards those that accept Christ as their Savior in the last minutes of their life with the same heaven as those that have been saved many years.

Interestingly, the Bible makes reference to Heaven thirty-four times and references Hell, Hades, and Sheol, a combined fifteen times, but there are *no* references to purgatory, or any place that would fit the Roman Catholic Church's definition of purgatory.

The doctrine of purgatory rests on the premise that while God forgives sin, His justice nevertheless demands that the sinner must suffer the full punishment due for his sin before he will be allowed to enter heaven. Such a distinction is illogical even according to human reasoning, for it would be unjust to forgive a criminal the guilt of his crime and still send him to prison to suffer for it. Nowhere in approved Scriptures do we find the concept of a place like purgatory. This is clearly a Catholic tradition that evolved after the time of Augustine.

Finally, the book of Hebrews confirms that after death there is *no* place to go for further purification, but rather there is immediate judgment. Mankind lives only once, and there is no second chance to earn salvation in a place called purgatory. "*And inasmuch as it is appointed for men to die once and after this comes the judgment*" (Hebrews 9:27). For Christians to be "absent from the body is to be 'spiritually' in the presence of the Lord," until the resurrection of their bodies, in the Second Coming of Christ. There is no provision in Scripture for a place of spiritual purification once we are dead. Our salvation to eternity depends on our personal decisions while we are alive on earth, and no amount of prayer from family or loved ones can save us from eternal punishment if we have not been made right with God before our death.

Statues, Relics, and Other Rituals—The Catechism of the Catholic Church says:

> All the signs in the liturgical celebrations are related to Christ: as are sacred images of the holy Mother of God and of the saints as well. They truly signify Christ, who is glorified in them. They make manifest the 'cloud of witnesses' who continue to participate in the salvation of the world and to whom we are united, above all in sacramental celebrations. Through their icons, it is man 'in the image of God,' finally transfigured 'into his likeness,' who is revealed to our faith. So too are the angels, who also are recapitulated in Christ: Following the divinely inspired teaching of our holy Fathers and the tradition of the Catholic Church (for we know that this tradition comes from the Holy Spirit who dwells in her) we rightly define with full certainty and

> Correctness that, like the figure of the life-giving cross, venerable and holy images of our Lord and God and Savior, Jesus Christ, our inviolate Lady, the holy Mother of God, and the venerate angels, all the saints and the just, whether painted or made of mosaic or another suitable material, are to be exhibited in the holy churches of God, on sacred vessels and vestments, walls and panels, in houses and on streets (CCC para. 1161).

To avoid the appearance of idolatry, however, no statues were placed in churches before A. D. 335 (*Short History of the Catholic Church,* p 65). It was the sixth century before statues and icons were developed and encouraged, and A.D. 787 before the approval of images and relics was authorized at the Second Council of Nicaea. Many fell into idolatry because they could not distinguish between the object and the spiritual idea. The Eastern Orthodox Church never accepted three-dimensional statues in churches because they were considered idols, and a reminder of the pagan Greek period of idol worship.

The Second Commandment of God is clear: "*You shall not carve idols for yourselves in the shape of anything in the sky above or the earth below or in the waters beneath the earth; you shall not bow down before them or worship them.*

For I, the Lord, your God am a jealous God, inflicting punishment for their fathers' wickedness on the children of those who hate me, down to the third and fourth generation; but bestowing mercy down to the thousandth generation, on the children of those who love Me and keep My Commandments" (Exodus 20:4–6).

Second Commandment Referring to Idol Worship Revised by the Catholic Church

The Catechism of the Catholic Church declares: "The division and numbering of the Commandments have varied in the course of history. The present catechism follows the division of the Commandments established by St Augustine, which has become traditional in the Catholic Church . . ." (CCC para. 2066).

Most Old Testament historians, however, place God's giving of the Ten Commandments to Moses on Mount Sinai in 1446 B.C. It is clear from Exodus 20:2–17, that the Second Commandment as recorded by Moses and given to the Israelites includes the words: *"You shall not carve idols for yourselves in the shape of anything in the sky above or the earth below..."*

The Apostolic Church of the first century followed the Old Testament division of the Ten Commandments in the same manner as Israel did, with the Second Commandment prohibiting "carved idols." Third century church father, Origen, listed the Ten Commandments in the same way as Israel and the apostles, by including the prohibition of "graven images," as the Second Commandment. It was only around A.D. 400 that Augustine devised a new division of the Ten Commandments that changed the emphasis away from "graven images," for the first time in some 1,850 years. Augustine moved some elements of the Second Commandment to the First; moved the Third Commandment, "You shall not take the name of the Lord your God in vain," to the Second Commandment; and split the Tenth Commandment into the Ninth and Tenth Commandments in order to have ten Commandments. (See CCC pages 496 and 497)

The issue for today's Catholics is: do you follow the Catholic Bible's emphasis on graven images, as recorded in Exodus and Deuteronomy, given by God Himself to Moses, which has been used by Jews and most non-Catholics for over 3,400 years, or do you follow the Catechism's revised version, which the Catholic Church has used since the time of Augustine? One can only guess Augustine's motivation for the revision, but as we noted above, no statues were placed in Christian Churches prior to A.D. 335.

The justification of statues in the Catholic Church is often explained as the mere honor or veneration of the saints whom these images represent. By definition, however, worship is expressed by actions such as bowing before the image, kneeling before it, crawling up to it, kissing it, affectionately touching it, praying to it, dressing it in fine clothes, burning candles before it, and offering it gifts.

Relics Are Classified by the Vatican as First, Second, or Third Class

The teaching of the Catholic Church with regard to the veneration of *relics* is summed up in a decree of the Council of Trent (Session XXV), which enjoins on bishops and other pastors to instruct their flocks that "the holy bodies of holy martyrs and of others now living with Christ"—which bodies were the living members of Christ and "the temple of the Holy Ghost" (1 Corinthians 6:19), and which are by Him to be raised to eternal life and to be glorified are to be venerated by the faithful, for though these [bodies] many benefits are bestowed by God on men.

Relics are classified by the Vatican as First Class, if they are body parts or blood of the saint; Second Class if they are items owned or used by the saint; and items merely touched by the saint are considered Third Class relics.

Gilles says:

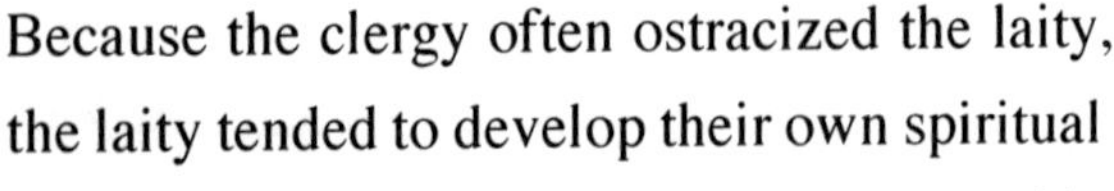

> Because the clergy often ostracized the laity, the laity tended to develop their own spiritual practices. Often such practices were at odds

> with official Church teaching, or at least, were on the fringes of orthodoxy. Such a practice was the trade in relics. Body parts or clothing of the martyrs were venerated in the early Church. Saint Augustine endorsed the honoring (though not the worshiping) of relics. With the return of the crusaders from the Holy Land, however, things got out of hand, as shiploads and cartloads of supposedly authentic remains of the apostles, the Virgin Mary, and the Lord Jesus Himself found their way West.

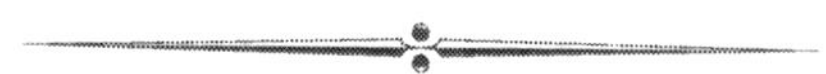

Gilles goes on to describe many scandals that came about as a result of the pent-up demand for relics, as relic hawkers came back from the Crusades, with anything that might resemble a relic of a saint, Christ, or the Virgin Mary. Towns and parishes would bargain for body parts and clothing from these saints. It got so ridiculous that sometimes many skeletons could be pieced together from bones owned by different towns and churches, supposedly of the same saint. One monastery claimed to display the baby teeth of Jesus, another the cross from Calvary reconstructed from many pieces of wood. Gilles, a Catholic and a historian, gives a very interesting account of many of the questionable practices of the Roman Catholic Church in the Middle Ages.

Finally, it would be a mistake to assume that the Catholic Church practices surrounding the veneration of relics was only a Middle-Ages phenomenon. "Relics of Pope John Paul II have enjoyed a boom ever since the beloved pope was beatified in 2011, and they were gaining heightened significance even ahead of canonization. "Relics of the two new saints (canonized together on April 27, 2014)—blood from Pope John Paul II that was used in his beatification ceremony of 2011 and a piece of skin from Pope John XXIII taken from his body as part of his 2000 beatification—were brought to an altar bedecked with thousands of roses from Ecuador" (*Wall Street Journal* 4/28/14).

Prayers to Mary and the Saints—The Catechism of the Catholic Church states, "'The Church's devotion to the Blessed Virgin Mary is intrinsic to Christian worship.' The Church rightly honors 'the Blessed Virgin with special devotion. From the most ancient times the Blessed Virgin has been honored with the title 'Mother of God,' to whose protection the faithful fly in all their dangers and needs. . . . This very special devotion . . . differs essentially from the adoration which is given to the incarnate Word and equally to the Father and the Holy Spirit, and greatly fosters this adoration.' The liturgical feasts dedicated to the Mother of God and Marian prayer, such as the rosary, an 'epitome of the whole Gospel,' express this devotion to the Virgin Mary" (CCC para. 971).

As for prayers to the Saints we read, "The witnesses who have preceded us into the kingdom, especially those whom the Church recognizes as saints, share in the living tradition of prayer by the example of their lives, the transmission of their writings, and their prayer today. They contemplate God, praise Him and constantly care for those whom they have left on earth. When they entered into the joy of their Master, they were 'put in charge of many things.' Their intercession is their most exalted service to God's plan. We can and should ask them to intercede for us and for the whole world" (CCC para. 2683).

There is no record of prayers to the saints or Mary in the Apostolic Church in the New Testament. St. Stephen was martyred before Saul, was converted and called Paul around A.D. 35. The Apostle James (the son of Zebedee) was martyred in A.D. 44, yet we know from Scriptures and other writings of the time that the apostles and their followers did not pray to these deceased saints or to Mary for intercession. Additionally, the apostles and their followers did not carve images or statues to venerate or to remember Mary or other deceased saints. Prayers to the deceased saints and to Mary began around A.D. 600 and long after the apostles were dead. The apostles did pray to God for each other in many places in Scripture, but in Scriptures they never prayed to the dead, or for the dead that had gone on before them. We also have the Old Testament record, which shows that the Old Testament believers did not pray to Abraham, Noah, Moses, or the prophets after they were dead, yet they were great men and saints of God.

Jesus tells us in the Scriptures that, "*I am the way, and the truth, and the life; No one comes to the Father, but through Me*" (John 14:6). "*God is One, One also is the mediator between God and men, the man Jesus Christ*" (1 Tim 2:5). "*There is no other name in the whole world given to men by which we are saved*" (Acts 4:11–12). To pray to anyone other than to Christ Himself for intercession with God the Father is forbidden in the Bible. Christians worship a jealous God!

It is illogical to think that He who died for us on Calvary is too busy to listen to our every prayer and need, or that we would get a better hearing from Christ if we had a mediator, like Mary, or a saint to make our case to Christ. We sell our Savior short by thinking that we would get more sympathy through the intercession of a deceased human.

VI

Marian Traditions in Roman Catholicism

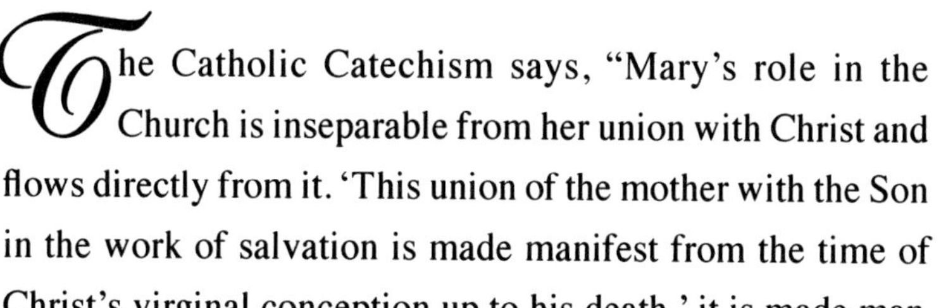

The Catholic Catechism says, "Mary's role in the Church is inseparable from her union with Christ and flows directly from it. 'This union of the mother with the Son in the work of salvation is made manifest from the time of Christ's virginal conception up to his death,' it is made manifest above all at the hour of his Passion" (CCC para. 964).

In his book, *Catholicism and Fundamentalism,* author and Catholic apologist Karl Keating claims, "In the Catholic scheme of things, she (Mary) is certainly different from other women, so much so that she is considered worthy of special devotion (not of course of worship 'he says,' *latria,* but of a level of honor, *hyperdulia,* higher than other saints receive)." Keating's statement would also be the official position of the Catholic Church, but in reality, the important question is, does the Catholic Church's day-to-day activities support this position? In other words, in the real world, does the Catholic

Church actually "honor" the Virgin Mary, or do they "worship" her?

To answer this question, we have to examine the main Traditions about Mary that the Catholic Church teaches and requires Catholics to believe, and then determine if these traditions represent "Honor or Worship." The American Heritage Dictionary defines honor and worship as follows:

Honor: "Special esteem or respect; reverence."

Worship: "The reverent love and allegiance accorded a deity, or sacred object. A set of ceremonies, prayers, or other religious forms by which love is expressed."

The Immaculate Conception—The Catholic Catechism reads, "To become the mother of the Savior, Mary 'was enriched by God with gifts appropriate to such a role.' The angel Gabriel at the moment of the annunciation salutes her as "full of grace." In fact, in order for Mary to be able to give the free assent of her faith to the announcement of her vocation, it was necessary that she be wholly borne by God's grace" (CCCpara. 490).

"Through the centuries the Church has become ever more aware that Mary, 'full of grace' through God was redeemed from the moment of her conception. This is what the dogma of the Immaculate Conception confesses, as Pope Pius IX proclaimed in 1854, 'The most Blessed Virgin Mary was, from the first moment of her conception, by a singular grace and privilege of almighty God and by virtue of the merits of Jesus Christ, Savior of the human race, preserved immune from all stain of original sin'" (CCC para. 491).

The Feast of the Immaculate Conception, celebrated on December 8, was established in 1476 by Pope Sixtus IV. The Immaculate Conception was solemnly and infallibly defined as a dogma by Pope Pius IX in his Constitution *Ineffabilis Deus,* on December 8, 1854, and is one of the six Holy Days of Obligation of the Catholic Church in the United States and is a public holiday in most Catholic countries.

The phrase "full of grace" is critical to the Immaculate Conception dogma. The New Testament was originally written in Greek, but this dogma is derived from the Latin Vulgate translation. In the original Greek, Luke 1:28 is translated, "*having gone into her he said rejoice one having been favored, the master is with you.*" "Full of grace" in Greek is "plaras karitos," and it occurs only two places in the New Testament, John 1:14; and Acts 6:8; neither verse is in reference to Mary. Therefore, the dogma of the Immaculate Conception was established on a flawed translation.

There is no Scripture verse in the Bible that says Mary was conceived without sin or that she lived a life free of sin. The only exception in the Bible of a person that was completely free from sin was Jesus Christ Himself. "*For our sakes He* (The Father) *made Him* (Christ) *to be sin who knew*

Nothing of sin, so that in Him we might become the very holiness of God" (2 Corinthians 5:21). We know that Mary was not sinless because the Bible very specifically says that no human has ever lived a sinless life. There are five very specific verses in the Bible that tell us this truth:

*(Ecclesiastes 7:20)- "*Yet there is no man on earth so just as to do good and never sin.*"

*(Romans 3:23)- "*All men have sinned and are deprived of the glory of God.*"

*(Romans 3:10-12)- "*There is no just man, not even one; there is no one who understands, no one in search of God. All alike have become worthless; not one of them acts uprightly, no, not one.*"

*(1 John 1:8)- "*If we say, 'we are free of the guilt of sin,' we deceive ourselves; the truth is not to be found in us.*"

*(Romans 5:12)- "*Therefore, just as through one man sin entered the world and with sin death, death thus coming to all men inasmuch as all sinned.*"

These verses are telling us that man is universally evil and that there is not a single person who has ever lived, apart from the sinless Lord Jesus Christ, whose innermost being could be characterized as righteous by God's perfect standard. To prevent people from thinking that there might be exceptions, Paul adds in Romans 3:12. *"no, not one."* The Good News of the gospel is that God provided Mary and all mankind throughout the ages a way to become perfect, divinely perfect, and that is only through the imputed righteousness of Christ. In God's sight, there are no levels of righteousness as far as salvation is concerned. There is either perfect righteousness in Jesus Christ or perfect sinfulness apart from Jesus Christ.

Many in the Catholic Church herself will readily admit to the flimsy evidence of the Immaculate Conception dogma. In, *A Handbook of the Catholic Faith,* by Van Doornik, published by Image Books in 1956; a book that carries the official Imprimatur (endorsement) of the Catholic Church; the author openly admits that there is no biblical authority for this curious dogma, as detailed in the following quote:

> This point of doctrine [the immaculate conception] is not expressly dealt with anywhere in the Bible, nor was it preached by the Apostles, and for many centuries it was not mentioned at all by the Church. Gradually, however, as the idea of the future dogma began to develop among the faithful, theologians submitted the point to the closest examination,

> and finally, the view then generally prevailing was formally pronounced as a dogma of the Church by His Holiness Pope Pius IX in 1854 (page 238).

This rather revealing Catholic statement about the Immaculate Conception not being biblical, unknown to the apostles, evolving over time, alien to the church for centuries, and having no higher spiritual authority than the pope and church councils, would have been unheard of in the first century church. The early church continued steadfastly in the doctrines of the apostles, and they practiced only that which was authorized by Christ.

"*They devoted themselves to the apostles' instruction and the communal life, to the breaking of the bread and the prayers*" (Acts 2:42), and Paul instructs the church at Colossae, "*Let the Word of Christ, rich as it is dwell in you. In wisdom made perfect, instruct and admonish one another. Sing gratefully to God from your hearts in psalms, hymns, and inspired songs. Whatever you do, whether in speech or in action, do it in the name of the Lord Jesus. Give thanks to God the Father through Him*" (Colossians 3:16–17).

It is clear from Scripture that Mary herself knew she needed a Savior to save her from her own sins when she says in Luke 1:47, "*My spirit finds joy in God my Savior.*" Like all mankind, Mary also needed a Savior! Even St

Thomas Aquinas (1225–1274), Supreme Theologian of the Roman Catholic Church, disagreed with the concept of the Immaculate Conception because of those very words that Mary herself spoke at the "Magnificat," ("God is my Savior"), in Luke 1:47. This Tradition of Mary being sinless contradicts Scripture and clearly goes beyond merely honoring Mary. It would appear that the concept of the Immaculate Conception with all of its celebration in the Catholic Church fits the definition of worship as opposed to just honor.

The Assumption—The Catechism of the Catholic Church states, "'Finally the Immaculate Virgin, preserved free from all stain of original sin, when the course of her earthly life was finished, was taken up body and soul into heavenly glory, and exalted by the Lord as Queen over all things, so that she might be the more fully conformed to her Son, the Lord of lords and conqueror of sin and death.' The Assumption of the Blessed Virgin is a singular participation in her Son's Resurrection and an anticipation of the resurrection of other Christians:

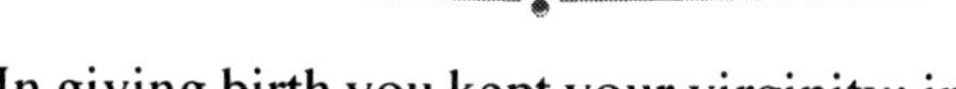

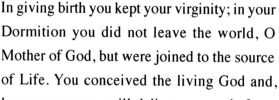

> In giving birth you kept your virginity; in your Dormition you did not leave the world, O Mother of God, but were joined to the source of Life. You conceived the living God and, by your prayers, will deliver our souls from death" (CCC para. 966).

Continuing in (CCC para. 969), "Taken up to heaven she did not lay aside this saving office but by her manifold intercession continues to bring us the gifts of eternal salvation. . . . Therefore the Blessed Virgin is invoked in the Church under the titles of Advocate, Helper, Benefactress, and Mediatrix." The Feast of the Assumption of the Blessed Virgin Mary is celebrated in the United States on August 15th and is one of only six official Catholic Church Holy Days of Obligation. This doctrine was dogmatically and infallibly defined by Pope Pius XII on November 1, 1950 in his Constitution, *Munificentissimus Deus*.

Catholics might ask doubters of the Assumption, why were Mary's bones not found, since relics of saints were honored in the early church? The simple answer is that only martyrs' relics were honored, and the earliest mention of a martyr's bones being venerated was Polycarp, after the New Testament, around A.D.156.

Biblical Record of Enoch and Elijah Being Assumed into Heaven, but Not Mary

Scripture does provide us with the names of two Old Testament saints who were taken bodily into heaven. In Genesis 5:24 we read, "*Enoch walked with God; and he was seen no more because God took him*." This event was confirmed in Hebrews 11:5 in the New Testament. The second person taken alive to heaven was the prophet Elijah, as described in 2 Kings 2:11, "*And as they went on, walking and talking together, behold a fiery chariot, and fiery horses parted them both asunder, and Elijah went up by a whirlwind into heaven.*" We also know that, "*No one has gone up to heaven except the One who came down from there—the Son of Man [who is in heaven]*" (John 3:13).

The problem with Mary's alleged assumption into heaven is that, unlike Enoch and Elijah, there is no confirmation in the Scriptures of what would have been a very important event in Christianity. The most likely person to report this event would have been the Apostle John, whom Christ asked to take care of His mother at the crucifixion. John took Mary into his home, so they were very close. We know that the Apostle John lived to a ripe old age and that he wrote the book of the Revelation around A.D. 94–96. Since John was the youngest apostle, it is safe to assume that he would have lived for a number of years after Mary died or was assumed into heaven, and it is inconceivable that such an important event, if it had occurred, would not have been reported by John. There is no scriptural basis for the "Assumption," so it is clearly a Catholic tradition and distinctly fits the definition of worship more than the definition of honor and is in direct opposition to Scripture that tells us, "*Empty is the reverence they do Me because they teach as dogmas mere human precepts. You disregard God's commandment and cling to what is human tradition*" (Mark 7:7, 8).

The Blessed "Virgin" Mary—The Catholic Catechism says the following about Mary's virginity: "The deepening of faith in the virginal motherhood led the Church to confess Mary's real and perpetual virginity even in the act of giving birth to the Son of God made man. In fact, Christ's birth 'did not diminish his mother's virginal integrity but sanctified it.' And so the liturgy of the Church celebrates Mary as *Aeiparthenos*, the 'Ever-virgin'" (CCC para. 499).

The Catholic doctrine of the perpetual virginity of Mary was well established by the fourth century and was supported by early theologians such as Ambrose, Jerome, Siricius and others. Unanimity, however, cannot be claimed about this doctrine as it was denied by important church leaders such as Tertullian. Tertullian, one of the greatest authorities in the ancient church, and who died in 222, raised his voice against the legend concerning Mary's birth. He also held that after the birth of Jesus, Mary and Joseph lived in a normal marital relationship. The famous preacher Chrysostom, who died in 407, resisted the "Mary movement" wholeheartedly, but his opposition had little long-term effect in stemming the movement.

During the Protestant Reformation, this doctrine came to be questioned because of the lack of clear biblical statements, and additionally there were no references to Mary as "ever virgin" in the Reformation creeds, even though early Reformation leaders such as Luther, Calvin, and Wesley believed in the veracity of this doctrine.

All the gospels, written long before the theory of Mary's perpetual virginity began to take hold of the popular imagination, had no qualms about Jesus having half-brothers and half-sisters. Luke, for instance says that Mary had more than one child: "*While they (Mary and Joseph) were there, the days of her confinement were completed. She gave birth to her firstborn son*" (Luke 2:6–7). Luke was writing after both Mary and Joseph were dead. If Jesus were Mary's only child, he would not have used the word "firstborn." Firstborn obviously implies that Mary had other children, which all the gospels confirm (see Mark 3:31–32; Matthew 12:46–50; John 2:12; John 7:3).

A reading of the Gospel shows that none of its authors ascribed a perpetual virginity to Mary. Matthew wrote specifically about the virgin birth and even implied that Mary had a normal relationship with her husband after the birth of Jesus. "*When Joseph awoke, he . . . took Mary home as his wife. But he had no relations with her at any time before she bore a son, whom he named Jesus*" (Matt 1:24–25).

Over the centuries, various Catholic theologians have tried many ways to reconcile the above Bible passages with Catholic theology. In one scenario, "James and Joseph, 'brothers of Jesus,' are the sons of another Mary, a disciple of Christ, whom St. Matthew significantly calls 'the other Mary'" (CCC para.500). In another scenario, the "brothers and sisters" mentioned in Scriptures were supposedly half-brothers and half-sisters of Jesus. They were supposedly stepbrothers and stepsisters from Joseph's earlier marriage. The problem with this belief is that nowhere in Scripture was it mentioned that Joseph was ever previously married. Additionally, this scenario also does not solve the problem with the implication of siblings in Luke 2:6–7.

Clear from Gospel Writers That Jesus Had Siblings

One question often posed by Catholics concerning the "Virgin Mary's" perpetual virginity centers around a passage in the gospels at the crucifixion. We read in John 19:26–27, "*Seeing His mother there with the disciple whom He loved (John), Jesus said to His mother, 'Woman, there is your son.' In turn He said to the disciple, 'there is your mother.' And from that hour the disciple took her into his care*." The point made by Catholics is, why would Jesus have given His mother to the disciple John if Jesus had bothers that would naturally have taken this responsibility?

We get a clue as to why Jesus chose John in the Gospel of Mark. Mark 3:32–35 reads, "*The crowd seated around Him told Him, 'Your mother and Your brothers and sisters are outside asking for you.' But He said to them in reply, 'Who are my mother and brothers?' And looking around at those seated in the circle He said, 'Here are my mother and my brothers. Whoever does the will of God is my brother and sister and mother to me.*'" It is clear that Jesus was making a decisive statement that discipleship involves a spiritual relationship that transcends the physical family. Couple this Scripture verse with John 7:5, which reads, "*Not even His brothers had much confidence in Him,*" and you begin to understand that Jesus did not give the responsibility of His mother to His brothers because they were not sympathetic to His ministry and did not believe in Him. Further, they likely were not even present at the time as their home was in Capernum.

As with the crowds in Jerusalem and Galilee, even His own brothers did not believe in Jesus at first. They did not become His followers until after the resurrection. We know that the following occurred early in the Book of Acts (after the resurrection). Acts 1:14 reads, "*Together they devoted themselves to constant prayer. There were some women in their company, and Mary the mother of Jesus, and His brothers.*" Further in Acts (15:13–22), James, brother of Jesus became leader of the Jerusalem church (see Gal. 2:9). Additionally, in reference to Jesus the psalmist wrote about Christ's relationship with his brothers in the Old Testament, "*Since for your sake I bear insult, and shame covers my face. I have become an outcast to my brothers, a stranger to my mother's sons*" (Psalm 69:8).

Another explanation often used by Catholics is that these brothers and sisters were not brothers and sisters but cousins. The assertion is that the Hebrew language lacks specific nouns for kinfolk. While true, there is one significant problem: all the four gospels were written in Greek, not Hebrew. In that language there are separate nouns for brothers and cousins. The Greek word for brother is *adelphoi* and for cousin is *anepsioi*. All the evangelist gospel writers, "who were inspired by the Holy Spirit," used *adelphoi* to describe his brothers. Had they been convinced that James, Joses, Judas, and Simon were not Jesus' brothers but cousins, they would clearly, "under the inspiration of the Holy Spirit," have used the word *anepsioi* to avoid any confusion, but they did not! Paul wrote in Greek, and he refers to Jesus' brothers in Galatians 1:18-19 and 1 Corinthians 9:4. There is absolutely nothing from Scripture to suggest that Mary remained a virgin perpetually. Perpetual virginity is clearly a Catholic tradition with no basis in the Bible and sets the Virgin Mary apart from humanity as an object of worship.

The Rosary – is described by the Catholic Catechism as "a prayer in honor of the Blessed Virgin Mary, which repeats the privileged Mariam prayer Ave Marie, or Hail Mary, in 'decades' of ten prayers, each preceded by the Pater Noster ('Our Father') and introduced by the Gloria Patri (Glory Be to the Father), accompanied by meditation on the mysteries of Christ's life. The rosary was developed in the Latin church as a popular substitute for the liturgical prayer of the Hours" (CCC page 897).

The rosary was invented by Peter the Hermit in 1090 and came into greater use in the thirteenth century when it was popularized by St. Dominic. A repetitive device similar to the rosary and used for counting prayers had been in use among the Buddhists and Muslims for centuries before the rosary was introduced, so its origin is not difficult to trace. The rosary has ten times as many prayers to Mary as to God the Father, thus exalting a human being more than God. The rosary represents a form of prayer that was expressly condemned by Christ, for He said: "*In your prayer do not rattle on like the pagans. They think they will win a hearing by the sheer multiplication of words. Do not imitate them*" (Matthew 6:7, 8). Not only does the rosary violate the Scriptures in terms of how we are to pray, but the rosary also puts Mary in front of God by the sheer number of prayers repeated specifically to Mary versus the number of prayers specifically devoted to God. Christ gave us His model prayer, the "Our Father," in Matt 6:9–13, not the "Hail Mary."

Catholic Church Tradition claims that Our Blessed Mother Mary promised Saint Dominic (1170–1221), and all who follow, "Whatever you ask in the Rosary will be granted." According to Catholic Tradition, the following are the Fifteen promises of the Rosary given by the Blessed Virgin to St. Dominic and to those who recite the "Holy Rosary."

1) *Whoever shall faithfully serve me by the recitation of the Rosary, shall receive single graces.*
2) *I promise my special protection and the graces to all those who shall recite the Rosary.*
3) *The Rosary will be a powerful armor against hell, it will destroy vice, decrease sin, and defeat heresies.*

4) *It will cause virtue and good works to flourish; it will obtain for souls the abundant mercy of God; it will withdraw the hearts of people from the love of the world and its vanities, and will lift them to the desire of eternal things. Oh, that souls would sanctify themselves by this means.*
5) *The soul which recommends itself to me by the recitation of the Rosary, Shall not perish.*
6) *Whosoever shall recite the Rosary devoutly, applying himself to the consideration of its Sacred Mysteries shall never be conquered by misfortune. God will not chastise him in His justice, he shall not perish by an un-provided death; if he be just, he shall remain in the grace of God, and become worthy of eternal life.*
7) *Whosoever shall have a true devotion for the Rosary shall not die without the Sacraments of the Church.*
8) *Those who are faithful to recite the Rosary shall have during their life and at their death the light of God and the plentitude of His graces; at the moment of death they shall participate in the merits of the Saints in Paradise.*
9) *I shall deliver from Purgatory those who have been devoted to the Rosary.*
10) *The faithful children of the Rosary shall merit a high degree of glory in Heaven.*
11) *You shall obtain all you ask of me by the recitation of the Rosary.*

12) All those who propagate the holy Rosary shall be aided by me in their necessities.

13) I have obtained from my Divine Son that all the advocates of the Rosary shall have for intercessors the entire celestial court during their life and at the hour of death.

14) All who recite the Rosary are my children, and brothers and sisters of my only Son, Jesus Christ.

15) Devotion of my Rosary is a great sign of predestination.

The Fifteen promises of the Rosary supposedly made to Saint Dominic by the Virgin Mary, and not refuted by the Catholic Church, are promises that can only be made by God Himself. Most require devotion and worship of the Virgin Mary, and clearly exalt the "Virgin Mary" as an object of worship through the Rosary. These promises are completely contrary to the teachings of Holy Scripture.

The Scapular—The Scapular was invented by Simon Stock, an English monk, in the year 1251. According to tradition, this holy man withdrew into the woods where he lived in great austerity for twenty years. At the end of the twenty years, he reported that the Virgin Mary, who appeared to him in celestial splendor, with thousands of angels, and holding the scapular in her hand, commissioned him to take this as the sign of the Carmelite Order to which he belonged. She proclaimed to him that, "Whosoever dies in this Scapular shall not suffer eternal fire."

The scapular consists of two pieces of brown cloth, usually wool, about four inches square, on which are pictures of the Virgin Mary. It is to be worn next to the skin suspended over the shoulders by cords fore and back. In 1943 the Carmelite National Shrine of Our Lady of Scapular in New York City, issued a circular entitled *The Scapular Militia,* with Cardinal Spellman's Imprimatur, which focused on Catholic service men at the height of World War II, and said in bold capital letters: "WHOSOEVER DIES CLOTHED IN THIS SCAPULAR SHALL NOT SUFFER ETERNAL FIRE" (*American Freedom and Catholic Power,* p. 248). Only God Himself can make a promise like the Virgin Mary reportedly made to Simon Stock. The Virgin Mary has been elevated by the Catholic Church to a status of deity with this claim. The Scriptures give us the only way to escape the fire, and it has nothing to do with wearing a scapular. It is repenting of our sins and accepting Jesus Christ as our Savior.

The Glories of Mary—The following quotes are taken from *The Glories of Mary*, 1931, written by Bishop Alphonse de Liguori, one of the greatest devotional writers of the Roman Catholic Church. Quotes *italicized* are from the Catholic Bible:

"And she is truly a mediatress of peace between sinners and God. Sinners receive pardon by...Mary alone" (pp. 82, 83). "He fails and is LOST who has not recourse to Mary" (p.94).

"God is one, One also is the mediator between God and men, the man Jesus Christ" (1 Tim 2:5). "Jesus told him: I am the way, and the truth, and the life; No one comes to the Father, but through Me" (John 14:6).

"The Holy Church commands a worship peculiar to Mary" (p.130). "Many things ...are asked from God, and are not granted; they are asked from Mary, and are obtained," for "She...is even Queen of Hell, and Sovereign Mistress of the Devils" (pp. 127,141,143).

"This Jesus is 'the stone rejected by you the builders which has become the cornerstone.' There is no other name in the whole world given to men by which we are to be saved" (Acts 4:11-12).

"The way of Salvation is open to none otherwise than through Mary," and since "Our salvation is in the hands of Mary... He who is protected by Mary will be saved, he who is not will be lost" (pp.169,170).

"I am the sheepgate. Whoever does not enter the sheepfold through the gate but climbs in some other way is a thief and

a marauder.....Whoever enters through Me (Christ) will be safe" (John 10:1,7,9). Also see (John 14:6) above. "Neither is there Salvation in any other" (Acts 4:12).

"All power is given to thee in Heaven and on earth," so that "at the command of Mary all obey-even God...and thus... God has placed the whole Church...under the domination of Mary" (pp. 180, 181).

"Full authority has been given to Me both in heaven and on earth. So that at Jesus' name every knee must bend in the heavens, on the earth and under the earth, and every tongue proclaim to the glory of God the Father: Jesus Christ is Lord!" "...so that primacy may be his in Everything" (Matt 28:18; Phil 2:9-11; Col. 1:18). "but if anyone Should sin, we have , in the presence of the Father, Jesus Christ, an Intercessor who is just. He is an offering for our sins, and not for our Sins only, but for those of the whole world" (1 John 2:1,2).

Liguori did more to promote the worship of Mary in the Roman Catholic Church than anyone historically, thereby enthroning Mary in the hearts of the people at the expense of dethroning Jesus Christ. Instead of excommunicating him for heresy, the Roman Catholic Church made him a cardinal for life and canonized him as a saint in death.

Apparitions of Mary—The Catechism of the Catholic Church describes an apparition as "an appearance to people on earth of a heavenly being—Christ, Mary, an angel, or a saint" (CCC page 867).

No study of the role of the Virgin Mary in the Roman Catholic Church could be complete without some comment on the many reports of the apparitions of Mary. Over the centuries scores of apparitions of Mary have been reported in various parts of the world. There are many shrines to Mary throughout the world. Three of the most famous examples of these are Fatima, Lourdes, and Guadalupe.

→Mary or an image of Mary appeared to a poor Native American, Juan Diego, at **Guadalupe** near Mexico City in 1531. She reportedly asked Juan Diego to tell people to build a temple in her honor and she would be their protector. An image of the lady in the apparition was miraculously left on the cloak of Juan Diego.

→In 1858, in **Lourdes**, France, 14-year-old Bernadette Soubirous claimed to see Mary, or an image of Mary. The apparition requested that Bernadette ask people to pray the rosary. Thousands of healings have been reported at Lourdes, but the Catholic Church officially claims very few. Over two million pilgrims make their way to Lourdes each year, many in search of the miraculous healing waters.

→Mary, or an image of Mary, appeared to three children ranging in age from 10 to 13 at **Fatima** in Portugal in 1917. The three children reported that the lady in the apparition appeared and shone more brilliantly than the sun. She held out her heart surrounded by thorns, which pierced it from all sides. She warned the children against the evils of communism, requested that they ask the people to pray the rosary every day for world peace, and to establish a devotion to the Immaculate Heart of Mary. 70,000 people at Fatima reportedly witnessed a whirling of the "sun in the sky" miracle. Mary, or an image of Mary, promised in the apparition to assist at the hour of death with "all the graces necessary for salvation, to all those who, on the first Saturday of five consecutive months, go to confession and receive Holy Communion, recite the rosary, and keep her company for a quarter of an hour while meditating on the mysteries of the rosary."

There is little question that in each of the above cases either Mary herself or some image of Mary appeared. With God nothing is impossible, and with Satan much is possible. Many witnesses testified to the validity of the events surrounding these three apparitions. If the apparitions were actually Mary, then there could be no doubt that the phenomena was from God. We know that the Mary of the Bible wanted to please and obey God. It would also be clear that whatever the message Mary delivered, it would have to be, without question, consistent with God's Word in Scripture. If the apparition was an "image" of Mary, it could be from God, or it could be from Satan.

The relevant question then becomes: Is Mary's message consistent with what God has revealed to us in the Scriptures?

God tells us that the Scriptures are sufficient and complete for our instruction in life and for our salvation. 2 Tim 3:15–17 says, "*Likewise, from your infancy you have known the sacred Scriptures, the source of the wisdom which through faith in Jesus Christ leads us to salvation. All Scripture is inspired of God and is useful for teaching-for reproof, correction, and training in holiness so that the man of God may be fully competent and equipped for every good work.*" This passage, along with many others in the Bible, (see Psalm 19:7–9), would declare that there is no further need of "new" divine revelation beyond God's Words in the Bible.

The apparitions all strongly emphasize praying the rosary, and special devotions to the Virgin Mary. Is this message consistent with God's Word on how we are to pray and worship?

The Word of God tells us that it is the will of God for Christians to pray to God the Father in the name of Jesus Christ. We see this in numerous Scriptures, such as, John

14:13, 14, which says, "*And whatever you ask in 'My' name, that 'I' will do, in order that the Father may be glorified in the Son. If you ask 'Me' anything in 'My' name, 'I' will do it.*" We also know from Scripture that Jesus Christ is the only mediator between God and man. Paul tells us in 1 Timothy 2:5, "*And the truth is this: God is One, One also is the mediator between God and men, the man Christ Jesus, who gave himself as a ransom for all.*" Further, we are given instruction on how not to pray in Matthew 6:7–9, "*In your prayer do not rattle on like the pagans. They think they will win a hearing by the sheer multiplication of words. Do not imitate them.*"

It is clear that for Christians to pray the rosary, with its strong focus on Mary—having fifty "Hail Mary's" to five "Our Fathers (Lord's prayer)," is a violation of God's instructions on praying only to God the Father, with Jesus as the only mediator. The rosary is a repetition of words, akin to the way pagans pray (see Matt 6:7–8). For Christians to follow the instructions of the image in the above apparitions would require amendments to much of the Bible, since the image requires the worship and adoration of her as opposed to, or in addition to, God. These "new revelations of Mary" manifested in the above apparitions are not consistent with God's Word. God alone wants, deserves, and demands all of the veneration, honor, and glory from all of humanity, with no exceptions. The word of God speaks of no salvation for anyone except through trusting in Jesus Christ alone.

We read in the Gospel of John, "*I am the way, and the truth, and the life; no one comes to the Father but through Me*" (John 14:6). We read in the book of Acts, "*There is no salvation in anyone else, for there is no other name in the whole world given to men by which we are to be saved*" (Acts 4:12). And, in the Book of Romans we read, "*Everyone who calls on the name of the Lord will be saved*" (Romans 10:13).

Mary is a human being and a believer. Like all other departed believers, her spirit is now with the Lord. Mary is not a goddess, and there is nothing to justify praying to her. In Scripture, there is absolutely no example of anyone praying to a dead saint. There is good reason for this: the human being who dies and goes to be with the Lord is still a human soul. Mary cannot hear and answer prayer. People who pray to Mary, though they say such prayers honor Mary, are actually, in fact, worshiping her as a type of deity.

We must always remember that Satan is the great deceiver. He will interject snippets of truth to achieve his deception. In the apparitions, you hear requests to pray for world peace, the evils of communism, and even healings. But the big lie is someone or something robbing God of the glory that is due Him alone. The real Mary of the Bible would never ask for veneration of herself as a substitute for, or in addition to, veneration of Almighty God.

It is also interesting to note that while many popes have visited the various shrines to Mary around the world and Pope John Paul II even once declared, "I am totally yours, Mary," neither he nor Pope Pius XII journeyed the relatively short distance to Lourdes for a miraculous healing when they were both very ill. They sought out the very best physicians in Europe for their medical care.

Holy Days of Obligation Devoted to Mary—"Principal feast days on which, in addition to Sundays, Catholics are obliged by Church law to participate in the Eucharist; a precept of the Church" (CCC page 882). "The precept of the Church specifies the law of the Lord more precisely: 'On Sunday's and other holy days of obligation the faithful are bound to participate in the Mass.' 'The precept of participating in the Mass is satisfied by assistance at a Mass which is celebrated anywhere in a Catholic rite either on the holy day or on the evening of the preceding day'" (CCC para. 2180).

Six such days are celebrated by the Catholic Church in the United States. Three of the six days are devoted specifically to the Blessed Virgin Mary: the Solemnity of Mary, Mother of God; the Immaculate Conception; and the Assumption. Two days are devoted specifically to Christ: the Ascension of Christ, and the Birth of Christ on Christmas day. The remaining day is devoted to All Saints' Day.

Catholic Church Calendar Days Devoted to Mary—The Catechism describes these feast days as, "The annual cycle of liturgical celebrations commemorating the saving mysteries of Christ's life, as a participation in the Paschal Mystery, which is celebrated annually at Easter, the 'Feast of feasts.' Feast days commemorating Mary, the Mother of God, and the saints are also celebrated, providing the faithful with examples of those who have been glorified with Christ" (CCC page 879).

Fifteen different feast days are devoted specifically to "honor" the "Virgin Mary" during a given year. In comparison, God the Father, Son, and Holy Spirit all combined are allotted only nine days.

Titles Assigned to Mary

Titles Assigned to the Virgin Mary by the Catholic Church:

Mother of God	Mother of Fairest Love
Mediatrix of All Graces	Mother of Divine Hope
Co-Redemtrix of Humanity	Mother of Unity
Queen of Heaven Queen	Mother of Mercy
Seat of Wisdom	Mother of Divine Providence
Mother of the Church	Mother of Consolation
Fountain of Salvation	Help of Christians
Mother of Good Counsel	Our Lady of Ransom
Cause of Our Joy	Queen of Peace
Pillar of Our Faith	Gate of Heaven

It is very clear that many of the above titles assigned by the Catholic Church to the Virgin Mary are titles encouraging worship and not titles of mere honor. Each of these titles could be easily challenged, but we will take two to make a point. We know that Mary does not appear in the Bible after Acts 1:12–14. This would nullify the idea of Mary as "Mother of the Church," as she appears to have had little if any role in the early church from Acts to Revelation.

The Catholic Church calls the Virgin Mary "Queen of Angels," "Mother of God," and "Queen of Heaven." Yet in Revelation 5:11–14, which focused on the end times and was written by the Apostle John around A.D. 100, after Mary was either assumed into heaven or died a natural death, we see absolutely no mention of Mary present with either the King of Heaven (the Father) on His throne, or with the Lamb of God (Jesus), who was standing with the Father. Certainly, John, who took care of Mary after Christ's death on the cross, would have reported Mary's presence if she had been in his vision of heaven. According to Catholic teaching, one would think that the "Mother of God" and the "Queen of Heaven" would be on her throne alongside the King of Heaven on His throne and next to Jesus, her son. Many Catholic Churches have statues of Mary with her heavenly crown as "Queen of Heaven," but she is nowhere to be found in this celestial scene in Revelation, when all the angels and the living creatures, myriads and myriads, and thousands of thousands are saying with a loud voice:

"*Worthy is the lamb that was slain to receive power and riches and wisdom and might and honor and glory and blessing.*

And every created thing, which is in heaven and on earth and under the earth and on the sea, and all things in them, I heard saying,

To Him who sits on the throne, and to the Lamb, be blessing and honor and glory and dominion forever and ever."

Some might come along and say that the woman in Chapter twelve of the Book of Revelation is the "Virgin Mary." Father John Echert, answering a question from a viewer on EWTN in December 2003, gave this explanation as to why the woman of Revelation must be Mary:

> The first level of "proof" would be the literal interpretation of the text itself, in which we see that this woman gives birth to a Son, whom the Dragon wishes to destroy. All commentators agree that the Son if Jesus Christ—and the Dragon is explicitly identified as Satan—therefore it is absolutely reasonable to assume that the Woman who gave birth to Jesus Christ MUST BE MARY, the Mother of our Lord.

The woman of Revelation Twelve, however, is described as a great sign appearing in heaven. She is not an actual woman, but a symbolic representation of Israel, pictured in the Old Testament as the wife of God (Isaiah 54:5-6). That this woman does not represent the church is clear from the context. She is clothed with the sun; moon under her feet, and with a crown of twelve stars. Being clothed with the sun speaks of the glory, dignity, and exalted status of Israel, the people of promise who will be saved and given a kingdom. The moon under her feet describe God's covenant relationship with Israel, since new moons were associated with worship (I Chronicles 23:31). The twelve stars represent the twelve tribes of Israel.

When a terrorist at the Vatican shot Pope John Paul II in 1981, he was heard saying over and over, "Mary save me, Mary save me." The leader of all the Catholics did not go to Jesus for help when his life was threatened, but rather he went to Mary. Yet, Jesus says in John 14:6, "*I am the way, and the truth, and the life; No one comes to the Father, but through Me*." John Paul II apparently trusted Mary's powers to save him more than Christ Himself. Did he not think that Christ could save him? It is clear Christ was not the Lord and Master of John Paul II's life, and Mary was.

Pope John Paul II dedicated himself and his Pontificate to "Our Lady." He bore the letter "M" for Mary in his coat of arms. His personal motto, which was embroidered on the side of his robes in Latin was the following: "Totus Tuus Sum Maria," which in English translates to: "Mary, I am all yours."

The *Los Angeles Times* ran the following story on September 1, 2002: "By awarding the "Virgin" (Mary) a central place in the cathedral (new $200mio. Structure in Los Angeles), the archdiocese is keeping faith with a long, if fluctuating, Catholic and Orthodox tradition of devotion to Our Lady, a tradition enjoying a resurgence under Pope John Paul II. (The pope's personal motto, 'Totus tuus sum Maria,' reflects his belief that the Virgin intervened to save his life from an assassin's bullet in 1981 so that he could help defeat European Communism)."

Summary—It would be rare to find an American Catholic who would say that they worship the Virgin Mary. One can only conclude, however, from the above Marian Traditions and the daily activities of Catholicism, and by the dictionary's definition of the word "worship," that millions of Catholics, knowingly or unknowingly, worship the Virgin Mary. The Catholic Church has special ceremonies for the Virgin Mary, prayers to her, images of her, statues of her, holy days assigned to her, titles of worship (Mother of God, Queen of Heaven) assigned to her, shrines named after her, and much more. Many of these Marian traditions are not optional but must be believed by a Catholic to be in good standing in the church with hope of eternal salvation.

As late as the fourth century there were no indications of any special veneration of Mary. Such veneration at the time could begin only if one was recognized as a saint, and only the martyrs were counted as saints. However, since there was no evidence that Mary had suffered a martyr's death, she was excluded from sainthood in the early church. The apostles never prayed to Mary, nor did they show her any special honor. Peter, Paul, John, and James do not mention her name once in the epistles which they wrote to the churches. John took care of her until she died, but he does not mention her in any of his three epistles or in the book of Revelation.

When the church was instituted at Pentecost, there was only one name given among men whereby we must be saved, that of Jesus (Acts 4:12). Nowhere in the Bible is there the slightest suggestion that prayer should be offered to Mary or the saints. If God had intended that we should pray to her, surely He would have instructed us to do so. Worship is accorded to the infant Jesus, but never to His mother. Jesus was careful to call Mary "woman," never "mother." Even when he was dying on the cross, He addressed her as "woman."

Christ had the perfect opportunity to elevate Mary as an object of veneration and worship in Luke 11:27, 28: "*While He was saying this a woman in the crowd called out 'Blest is the womb that bore you and the breasts that nursed you!' Rather, He replied. 'Blest are they who hear the Word of God and keep it.*'" Note that Christ did just the opposite by not conferring on Mary any greater honor than the blessedness of those who hear and obey the Word of God.

The relationship between Jesus and Mary is often compared by Catholics to the emotional and sentimental bond that they share with their own earthly mothers. It is often said that mothers are the only person in life that love their children unconditionally, and that they would do almost anything for their children. Catholics often apply this human reasoning to Mary's relationship with Jesus, assuming that Jesus will not turn down a request from Mary if they just pray to her, rather than to Christ. Christians consider Mary blessed, but not a deity able to answer prayer. Mormons worship a mother god, but Christians do not. To assign the sentimentality associated with our earthly mothers to Mary's relationship with Christ is not to understand the divine nature of God, who demands all of our prayers and all of our undivided devotion and worship.

In many ways the Virgin Mary has been elevated to the level of a deity in the Catholic Church and has no relationship to the real Mary of the Bible. The Mary of the Bible is to be loved and respected by all for the significant role she played in the life of our Lord. But to worship Mary or any other saint is a clear violation of God's law. Only God is to be worshiped! God demands all our praise! "*I am the Lord, this is My name; My glory I give to no other*" (Isaiah 42:8). "*God is to receive all our praise*" (Psalm 115). It does not say that God "and Mary" are to receive all of our praise. In Revelation 22:8, John fell down to worship an angel, but the angel said, "*No, get up! I am merely a fellow servant with you and your brothers the prophets and those who heed the message of this book. Worship God alone!*" The angel did not say to worship God "and Mary."

Prayer Is One of the Deepest Forms of Worship

While most Catholics would deny that they worship Mary, and the Catholic Church herself denies that she encourages the worship of Mary, still it is clear that the Catholic Church has cast "Mary" in the role of the greatest human that ever lived, and worthy of "worship," in spite of the Scriptures telling us something entirely different. In Matthew 11:11, Christ Himself says, "*I solemnly assure you, history has not known a man* (human) *born of woman greater than John the Baptizer,*" but John the Baptist was never worshiped by the Christian Church.

Prayer is one of the deepest forms of worship because prayer acknowledges the full power of the person to whom we pray. It is likely that millions of people all over the world are praying to Mary at the same time, in many different languages, and asking for a great variety of things. In order for Mary to hear and answer all those prayers, Mary would have to be omnipresent, omniscient, and omnipotent, which are qualities that only God possesses. It is clear that people who pray to Mary, even though they might consider this venerating or honoring, are in fact, by definition, worshiping her.

The very fact that the Catholic Church claims that Mary is the Mother of God, immaculately conceived without sin, a perpetual virgin; Co-Redemtrix of the Universe, Mediatrix of all Grace; was assumed into heaven; Has three Holy Days of Obligation in her honor, when Christ has only two; has fifteen feast days each year on the Catholic Calendar, when God the Father, Son, and Holy Spirit combined have only nine days; has shrines devoted to her all over the world, has statues in all Catholic Churches, and is called Queen of Heaven by the Catholic Church; all declare that Mary has achieved Godhood, in the eyes of Roman Catholicism, in spite of the official denial of the Roman Catholic Church.

The Mary of the Bible

It should be confounding for Catholics to note that Mary, the mother of Jesus, is mentioned only five times in the Bible after the birth of Christ (Matt 2:13–18; Luke 2:41–52; Jn. 2:1–12; Jn. 19:26; and Acts 1:14). There is no record of the apostles seeking Mary's advice. Mary taught no doctrines that were reported. There is no biblical record of any leadership role for Mary. This modest reference in the Bible is in stark contrast to the dominant role that the Virgin Mary plays in the Roman Catholic Church today. This is a great illustration of why Scripture must always take precedence over tradition.

We have to thank God for Mary and rejoice because of her. We consider her blessed. Mary is definitely a shining example of how we, as believers, should live. She exemplifies genuine faith, dedication, purity, humility, perseverance, self-denial, and suffering for the sake of Christ. She was knowledgeable of the Scriptures and obedient to its precepts. However, we must not extol Mary beyond her role as a believer. Mary would want us to follow God's Word and to focus on Christ and trust Him as our only mediator.

VII

Scripture versus Tradition

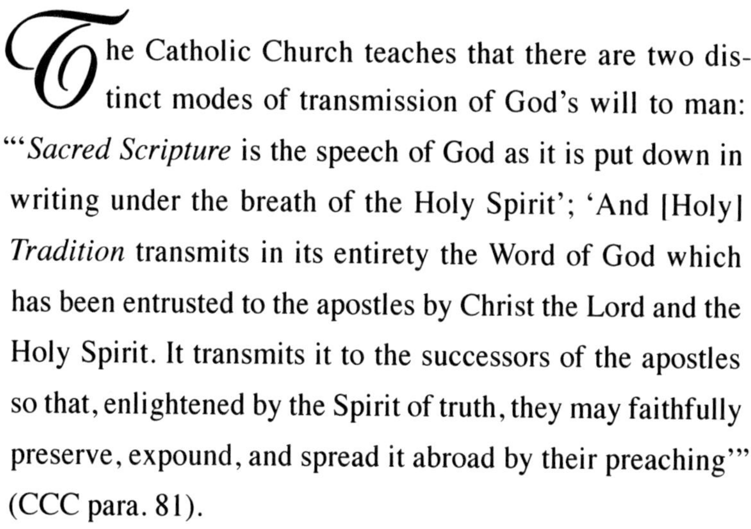

The Catholic Church teaches that there are two distinct modes of transmission of God's will to man: "'*Sacred Scripture* is the speech of God as it is put down in writing under the breath of the Holy Spirit'; 'And [Holy] *Tradition* transmits in its entirety the Word of God which has been entrusted to the apostles by Christ the Lord and the Holy Spirit. It transmits it to the successors of the apostles so that, enlightened by the Spirit of truth, they may faithfully preserve, expound, and spread it abroad by their preaching'" (CCC para. 81).

Further, according to the Catechism, "As a result the Church, to whom the transmission and interpretation of Revelation is entrusted, 'does not derive her certainty about all revealed truths from the Holy Scriptures alone. Both Scripture and Tradition must be accepted and honored with equal sentiments of devotion and reverence'" (CCC para. 82).

In a search for truth, however, we must separate those beliefs that are clearly based on Scripture and are divinely inspired by God Himself, from those beliefs that are man-made traditions. The danger in not doing so is that the man-made traditions will often nullify the very truths in the Bible that God has divinely revealed to man and to which He wants man to adhere.

Christ reserves His harshest criticism in all of Scriptures toward man-made tradition. The Pharisees and Sadducees, who were the most outwardly spiritual of all the Jews, had established many dietary laws, certain ceremonies, and religious articles that were man-made traditions and not part of Old Testament Law. In Matthew 15:6–9, Christ says to these "most religious" Jews, ". . . *This means that for the sake of your tradition you have nullified God's Word. You hypocrites! How accurately did Isaiah prophesy about you when he said: 'This people pays me lip service but their heart is far from me. They do me empty reverence, making dogmas out of human precepts.'*" Mark 7:8–9 states, "*You disregard God's commandment and cling to what is human tradition.* He went on to say: *you have made a fine art of setting aside God's commandment in the interests of keeping your traditions.*"

At Trent the Catholic Church Declared Tradition Equal with Scripture

By the time of the Council of Trent in 1546, many Catholic doctrines had strayed so far from divine revelation in the Scriptures that it was necessary for the leadership of the Catholic Church to place Roman Catholic tradition on the same level as Holy Scripture to justify the numerous traditions that could not be justified by the Scriptures.

In 1546, at the Council of Trent, the Catholic Church declared man-made Catholic Church tradition equal with divine revelation in Scripture. With one stroke of the pen, the Catholic Church gave herself the authority to decide what man-made beliefs she would follow without the obligation of adhering to a scriptural authority. The overall effect of this decision was to subordinate God's Word to Catholic Church Tradition; thereby putting the Mass, Transubstantiation, Confession, Purgatory, exaltation of Mary, Indulgences, and other doctrines on an equal level, and in many cases in front of preaching the Gospel and the study of God's Word as revealed in the Bible.

Focusing on these numerous traditions, by definition, is at the expense of God's Law in the Scriptures. And what is Christ's response? "*When that day comes, many will plead with Me, 'Lord, Lord, have we not prophesied in your name? Have we not exorcised demons by its power? Did we not do many miracles in your name as well?' then I will declare to them solemnly, I never knew you. Out of my sight, you evil-doers*" (Matt. 7:22, 23)! What is the evil that Christ is referring to in this passage? The evil is man's rebellion against the Law of God. Another translation of the above is "*depart from me you who practice lawlessness*." Man refuses to learn the Law (Scriptures), and man refuses to live by God's divine revelation, which is contained in the Bible. Any religious practices that do not include a scriptural basis are "lawlessness."

Some have even gone as far as to say that because Christ never wrote down anything Himself, that all is tradition, and that the Holy Spirit directs the Catholic Church to determine what is doctrine and what is not doctrine. Christ's life on earth, however, was Divine Tradition that was Scripture in the making. Christ, before His Resurrection promised the apostles that the Holy Spirit would help (inspire) them to remember His words and deeds. In the Book of John, Christ tells the apostles, "*The Paraclete, the Holy Spirit, whom the Father will send in My name will instruct you in everything and remind you of all that I told you*" (John 14:26).

The Eternal Security of the Believer

One of the important differences between Roman Catholic tradition and Protestant biblical beliefs is in the eternal security of the believer. In Catholicism one's security is uncertain until death, and still usually requires further payment for sin after death, even if the person has obeyed all of the Catholic

Church's doctrines and rules to the best of their ability. The tradition of venial and mortal sin, confession, indulgences, and purgatory play an important role in the Catholic concept of a "process of justification or salvation," which may entail gaining and losing one's salvation numerous times over a Catholic's lifetime. Grace to do good is dispensed by Mass and the sacraments, as the parishioner takes advantage, over time, of opportunities to receive this grace. Catholics believe that Baptism was given to take away the sin inherited from Adam (original sin) and any sins they personally committed before baptism. For sins committed after baptism, a different sacrament is needed; it is called the sacrament of reconciliation, penance, or confession.

It seems unfair in man's economy that through no fault of our own each of us has inherited the DNA sin nature of depravity and guilt from a distant relative, one man: Adam. In the same way in God's economy it seems too good to be true that through one man, the God man Christ, we should inherit the DNA of freedom from sin and guilt as a free gift, with no strings attached, except to have faith in Him who gives us that freedom. In some sense this thinking parallels the difference between Catholic tradition and biblical Christianity. The apostle Paul summarizes this with the analogy between Adam and Christ in the following passages in the Book of Romans: "*To sum up, then: just as a single offense brought condemnation to all men, a single righteous act brought all men* (who exercise faith in Christ) *acquittal and life. Just as through one man's disobedience all became sinners, so through one man's obedience all shall become just. The law* (10 Commandments) *came in order to increase offenses; but despite the increase of sin, grace has far surpassed it, so that, as sin reigned through death, grace may reign by way of justice leading to eternal life through Jesus Christ our Lord*" (Romans 5:18–21).

The apostle Paul describes his own human condition, and that of every believer in the following passages from the Book of Romans: *"We know that the law is spiritual, whereas I am weak flesh sold into the slavery of sin. I cannot even understand my own actions. I do not do what I want to do but what I hate. When I act against my own will, by that very fact I agree that the law is good. This indicates that it is not I who do it but sin which resides in me. I know that no good dwells in me, that is, in my flesh; the desire to do right is there but not the power. What happens is that I do, not the good that I will to do, but the evil that I do not intend. But if I do what is against my will, it is not I who do it, but sin which dwells in me. This means that even though I want to do what is right, a law that leads to wrong doing is already at hand. My inner self agrees with the law of God, but I see in my body's members another law at war with the law of my mind; this makes me the prisoner of the law of sin in my members. What a wretched man I am! Who can free me from the body under the power of death? All praise to God, through Jesus Christ our Lord! So with my mind I serve the law of*

God but with my flesh the law of sin" (Romans 7:14-25). Paul is telling us that even the most spiritual and mature believer, when they honestly evaluate themselves against the righteous standard of God's law, realize how far short they fall. It is impossible for man on his own to win the battle against his flesh and the world, but God has provided a way, through Jesus Christ, for man to be victorious, through God's Spirit dwelling within him.

No Sin a Believer Can Commit Can Be Held against Him

In the Bible, one's eternal security is affirmed at the point in time that one repents and believes that Jesus is the Son of God. The new believer receives the Holy Spirit and the continuous grace to live the Christian life. This one-time and permanent eternal security of the believer is captured in the Book of Romans, when the apostle Paul writes, "*There is no condemnation now for those who are in Christ Jesus. The law of the Spirit, the Spirit of Life in Christ Jesus, has freed you from the law of sin and death*" (Romans 8:1). This verse summarizes the counter intuitive results of the first seven chapters of Romans: that justification is by faith alone on the basis of God's overwhelming grace. No sin a believer can commit—past, present, or future—can be held against him, since Christ paid the penalty in full and righteousness was imputed (credited) to the believer. And no sin will ever reverse this divine legal decision. God's true children are free from the bondage of sin; they have been redeemed! This freedom does not give the believer a license to sin, as some might suggest, God forbid, but rather the grace to avoid living a life in sin. Through the indwelling of the Holy Spirit God has given man a new regenerated heart that changes the believer's desires toward wanting to please God, rather than oppose God.

The apostle Paul powerfully reaffirms this truth of the eternal security of the believer again, in no uncertain terms, beyond any doubt, at the end of Romans 8:

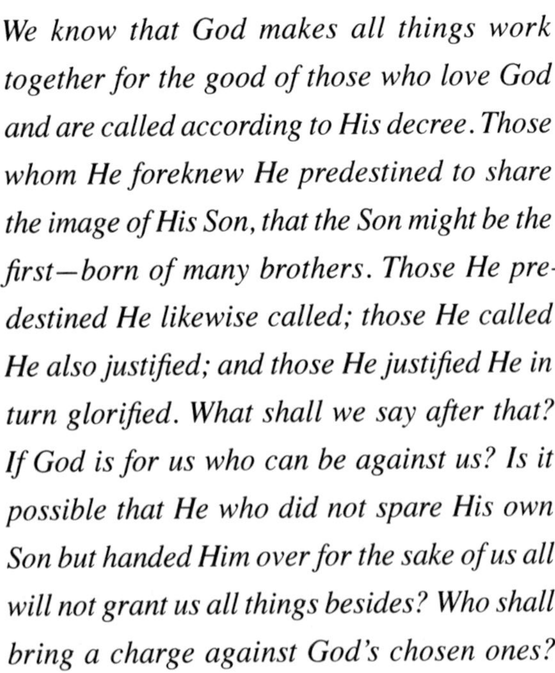

> *We know that God makes all things work together for the good of those who love God and are called according to His decree. Those whom He foreknew He predestined to share the image of His Son, that the Son might be the first—born of many brothers. Those He pre-destined He likewise called; those He called He also justified; and those He justified He in turn glorified. What shall we say after that? If God is for us who can be against us? Is it possible that He who did not spare His own Son but handed Him over for the sake of us all will not grant us all things besides? Who shall bring a charge against God's chosen ones?*

> *God, who justifies? Who shall condemn them? Christ Jesus, who died or rather was raised up, who is at the right hand of the Father and who intercedes for us? Who will separate us from the love of Christ? Trial, or distress, or persecution, or hunger, or nakedness, or danger, or the sword? . . . For I am certain that neither death nor life, neither angels nor principalities, neither the present nor the future, nor powers, neither height nor depth nor any other creature will be able to separate us from the love of God that comes to us in Christ Jesus, our Lord* (Romans 8:28–39).

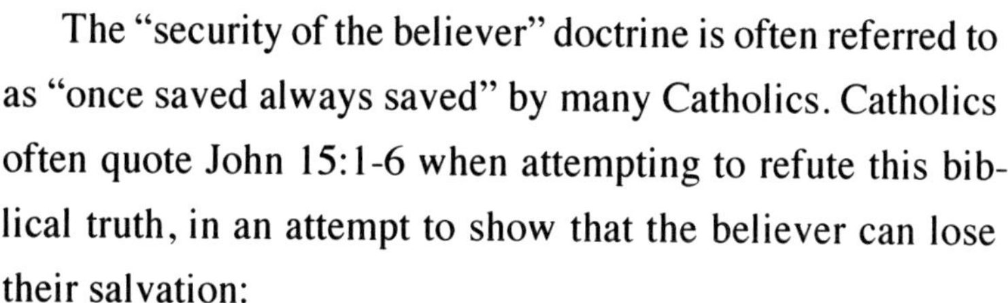

The "security of the believer" doctrine is often referred to as "once saved always saved" by many Catholics. Catholics often quote John 15:1-6 when attempting to refute this biblical truth, in an attempt to show that the believer can lose their salvation:

> *I am the true vine, and My Father is the vinegrower. He prunes away every barren branch, but the fruitful ones he trims clean to increase their yield. You are clean already, thanks to the word I have spoken to you. Live on in me,*

> *as I do in you. No more than a branch can bear fruit of itself apart from the vine, can you bear fruit apart from me. I am the vine, you are the branches. He who lives in me and I in him, will produce abundantly, for apart from me you can do nothing. A man who does not live in me is like a withered, rejected branch picked up to be thrown into the fire and burnt.*

In this extended metaphor, however, Christ is saying that the branches that bear fruit are genuine believers. The branches that do not bear fruit are those who profess to believe, but their lack of fruit indicates that genuine salvation has never taken place and they have no life from the vine. This imagery extends from him to all those who make a profession of faith in Christ but do not actually possess salvation. We see this idea also expressed in the parable of the soils (Matthew 13:5-6). The seed that fell on rocky soil, and immediately sprang up, but withered away, because it had no roots. Judas, is an example of one who professed to believe, but did not. *"It was from our ranks that they took their leave – not that they really belonged to us; for if they had belonged to us, they would have stayed with us. It only served to show that none of them was ours"* (1 John 2:19).

Another often quoted passage of Scripture that is used to try to claim that a believer can lose their salvation is Galatians

5:1-5, which reads, *"It was for liberty that Christ freed us. So stand firm, and do not take on yourselves the yoke of slavery a second time. Pay close attention to me, Paul, when I tell you that if you have yourself circumcised Christ will be of no use to you. I point out once more to all that receive circumcision that they are bound to the law in its entirety. Any of you who seek your justification in the law have severed yourself from Christ and fallen from God's favor! It is in the spirit that we eagerly await the justification that we hope for, and only faith can yield it. In Christ Jesus neither circumcision nor the lack of it counts for anything; only faith, which expresses itself through love. You were progressing so very well; who diverted you from the path of truth?"*

The Greek word for "severed" means "to be separated," or "to be estranged." The word for "fallen" means "to lose one's grasp on something." Paul's clear meaning is that any attempt to be justified by the law is to reject salvation by grace alone through faith alone. Those once exposed to the gracious truth of the gospel, who then turn their backs on Christ and seek to be justified by the law are separated from Christ and lose all prospects of God's gracious salvation. Their desertion of Christ and the gospel only proves that their faith was never genuine.

Yet another passage used by those that would claim that a believer's salvation can be lost reads, *"If some of the branches were cut off and you, a branch of the wild olive tree, have been grafted in among the others and have come to share in the rich root of the olive, do not boast against the branches. If you do boast, remember that you do not support the root; the root supports you. You will say, 'Branches were cut off that I might be grafted in.' Well and good. They were cut off because of unbelief and you are there because of faith. Do not be haughty on that account, but fearful. If God did not spare the natural branches, he will certainly not spare you"* (Romans 11:17-21).

In these verses Paul is warning the Romans of their arrogance and unbelief; if Israel's special calling and blessing from the Lord could not protect them from being broken off, then certainly the Gentiles lack of that calling and blessing cannot protect them from being broken off for their unbelief. Paul gave a similar warning to the church at Corinth (1 Corinthians 10:12). Paul realized that just as was true in Corinth, Pergamum, and Laodicea; the Roman church also had a percentage of apostates, heretics, and others who had a false faith, some even denying the deity of Christ. The only issue is faith. The Jews were cut off because of unbelief, and the Gentiles were grafted in on the basis of their faith in the Lord Jesus Christ. Paul had no precise way of knowing who in the Roman church had saving faith and who did not, but even the true believers in the Roman church often had attitudes of Gentile superiority towards Jewish converts to Christ, which Paul wanted to discourage. Paul warns even those who have identified with the saving gospel that they must persevere in the kindness of Christ, or they will be judged and punished, by a loving Father. This punishment, however, was not a loss of their salvation, but some worldly punishment that God would impose upon them, as the result of sin.

Some might even come along and say that the "assurance of salvation" is a modern invention of John Calvin introduced at the time of the Protestant Reformation (circa 1517), and not part of the teaching of the early church. In a sense they would be right, inasmuch as the Catholic Church did not teach this doctrine in her earlier years, and that the term "assurance of salvation" is not in the Bible and it is relatively modern, much as is true of the term the "Trinity" which is also not in the Bible. The idea of the believer being assured that once they accepted Christ as their Savior, that Christ would not leave them, however, was taught as part of the gospel "Good News" in the Christian Church of the first century. The concept of this doctrine was written about and preached by the apostle Paul in the Book of Romans (Romans 8:1; 8:28-39), written in A.D. 56, and written about and preached by the apostle John in the Book of John (John 6:37; 6:39-40), written in A.D. 90-95 .The fact of the matter is that Calvin, Luther, and the other reformers did not invent a new doctrine, they simply returned to the original teachings of the first century Christian Church of the apostles concerning the believer's assurance of salvation.

Many Catholics quickly dismiss any biblical challenge to Catholic tradition as just anti-Catholic rhetoric, and not worthy of their consideration. It is very difficult for many

Catholics to objectively consider any critique of the Catholic Church or her teachings even if the critiques are historically and biblically justified. Much of this defensive mindset goes back to generational loyalty to the faith of parents, grandparents, and even great-grandparents. If you have been taught from birth by those that love you, and that you love, that you were fortunate to be born and baptized into "The One True Church," which is the only path to eternal salvation, and this message has been reinforced systematically by your family, by the parochial school you attend, and the church where you attend Mass, this often produces a fierce loyalty to your church and a faith that is ultimately in your church as an authority figure more than in Christ. The parish priest was historically held in the highest esteem, as the representative of Christ, and was seldom questioned by parishioners on his preaching, teaching, or personal life. In this environment it is difficult to get exposure to a different point of view, other than by the work of the Holy Spirit.

The Catholic Church's Index of Prohibited Authors and Books

Over the centuries, this ideology was strengthened by the Catholic Church's Index of Prohibited Authors and Books. Many books were banned, especially those that were deemed as threats to Catholic teachings. Although formally abolished in 1966 by Pope Paul VI, over nearly four centuries church leaders flagged more than 4,000 works as damaging to the faith or morals of Catholics—and threatened excommunication for reading, publishing, selling, or even possessing them. The Vatican's Congregation for the Doctrine of the Faith still reserves the right to ban books "it deems" theologically erroneous. But sometimes the church changes its mind.

"The 16th-century Dominican Friar Giordano Bruno, an astronomer burned at the stake for, among other things, asserting that the sun was just one of a number of heavenly bodies, is now honored with a monument in Rome. The writings of St. Faustina Kowalska, a Polish mystic who founded the Divine Mercy devotion, were on the Index for 20 years.

"These reversals call into question the value of such censorship, which at the very least damages the church's image in modern society" (October 2010 issue of *U.S. Catholic* by Heidi Schlumpf [V0175, No. 10, page 46)]). As an aside, it is curious how books such as, *To Kill a Mockingbird*, the Bible, *Les Miserables*, and *The Hunchback of Notre Dame*, could be on the index, yet Hitler's *Mein Kampf* escaped the infamous index list of banned books.

One of the most exhaustive studies of the differences between Scripture and tradition was penned in 1962 by Princeton theologian, Dr. Loraine Boettner (1901–1990). Catholics have criticized *Roman Catholicism* for over fifty years as being anti-Catholic, because of the harsh tone of its author toward Catholic traditions and beliefs. Some of Boettner's criticisms, like the Mass in Latin, were vindicated by Vatican II. It is unfortunate that Boettner's antagonistic approach to Catholicism diminished some of the otherwise scholarly and historical value of his work, which was supposedly written to be helpful to Christians who were seeking to understand the difference between biblical Christianity and the traditions of Catholicism.

The Council of Trent, which was in session from 1545 to 1563, was a major turning point in the Catholic Church's commitment to protecting the church's human traditions from the scrutiny of Scripture, by pronouncements of anathemas. Scores of anathemas (condemnations) arose from Trent against anyone who dared not to believe key Catholic traditions and beliefs, many of which were in contradiction to the Scriptures, or not mentioned in Scripture at all. Traditions such as indulgences, justification by faith plus works, infant baptism, and purgatory became dogmas of Catholicism, and Trent laid the foundation for dogmatizing future traditions like the Assumption, the Immaculate Conception, papal infallibility, Mary as co-redeemer with Christ, and many others which were not biblically based.

The Bible tells us that, "*Your rebirth has come, not from a destructible but from an indestructible seed, through the living and enduring Word of God*" (1 Peter 2:23).

Paul writes, "*Brothers, I want to remind you of the gospel I preached to you, which you received and in which you stand firm. You are being saved by it at this very moment if you hold fast to it as I have preached it to you. Otherwise you have believed in vain. I handed on to you first of all what I myself received, that Christ died for our sins in accordance with Scriptures; that He was buried and, in accordance with the Scriptures, rose on the third day*" (1 Corinthians 15:1–3).

VIII

True Christianity

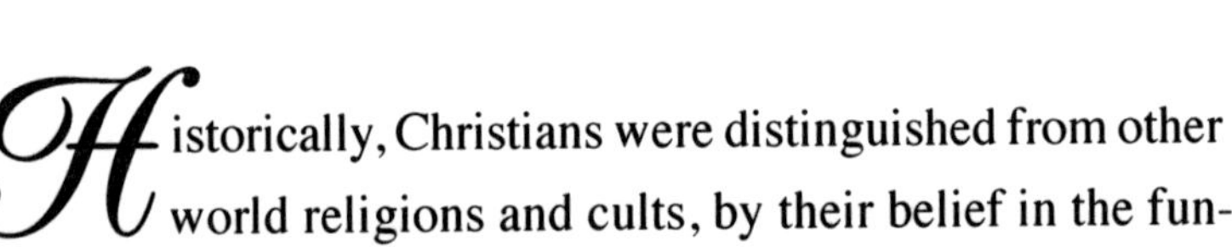

Historically, Christians were distinguished from other world religions and cults, by their belief in the fundamental creeds of the first century apostles, which were four primary beliefs:

* The virgin birth
* The Trinity
* The deity of Christ
* The Resurrection

If a church, a denomination, or an individual believed in these four creeds, then they were considered professing Christians. The critical issue, however, is what determines a true saved Christian, as it is clear the many of the world's two billion "professing Christians" are not true believers, but are "tares" within the local churches.

The Book of Revelation Is a Key to Christ's "One True Church"

As mentioned in the introduction; in the first three chapters of the Book of Revelation we are presented with a picture of this reality of "wheat and tares" in the church. Five of the seven "Christian Churches" (70+ percent) that the apostle Paul himself had founded in Asia-Minor on his first two missionary journeys—Ephesus, Pergamun, Thyatria, Sardis, and Laodicea—were all in some level of apostasy by A.D. 100. The degree of this apostasy was determined by how far they had strayed from their original and singular devotion to Christ and Christ alone, "their first love." As these churches added additional false teachings to the true gospel that Paul had given them, they moved further away from Christ, and deeper into apostasy and needed reform. Within these five churches, however, there were some who did not follow the false teachers but continued believing in the true gospel, and these individuals in each of the five churches in apostasy, represent the true and saved believers in the body of Christ, or Christ's true church.

These seven churches are prototypes of Christian Churches even today. While we cannot know for certain, because only God knows, it is still reasonable to assume that today 70 percent, or more, of the world's Christian Churches and many of their members could be unsaved, but still be professing Christians. This notion seems to be confirmed by the following Bible passage: "*Enter through the narrow gate.*

The gate that leads to damnation is wide, the road is clear, and many choose to travel it. But how narrow is the gate that leads to life, how rough the road, and how few there are who find it" (Matthew 7:13).

True Christianity is not a church denomination, or a religion, or an "ism," but rather a personal relationship between God and man. True Christians make up what has been called the "Body of Christ" since apostolic times. Christianity began with Christ and the Gospel Good News that was preached by the apostles and their disciples.

In an October 2010 open letter to the Billy Graham Evangelical Association, Franklin Graham wrote:

> So what is a Christian? Jesus said that His true followers are those who have been born again by the Spirit of God. When a Jewish religious leader named Nicodemus came to talk with Jesus one night, he declared that God was with Jesus because of all the miraculous signs that Jesus performed. Jesus had this penetrating response: '*I tell you the truth, no one can see the kingdom of God unless he is born again. . . . Flesh gives birth to flesh, but the Spirit gives birth to spirit*' (John 3:3, 6 NIV).

We Must Be Born Again

Graham continues, "The phrase 'born again' in Scripture literally means 'to be born from above'—a spiritual rebirth. A Christian is a man, woman, or child who has experienced a spiritual new birth through the regenerating work of the Holy Spirit. That new birth is a gift of God, through Jesus Christ, given by the grace He freely offers to all."

Finally, Graham writes:

> Some believe you can be born into a faith. For example, a child born to Muslim parents is considered a Muslim by many people. A son or daughter born to a Jewish mother is typically considered to be Jewish, and someone born into a Christian family is often assumed to be a Christian. No one, however, is ever automatically a Christian by birth. To be a Christian, you must make a conscious choice to turn from your sins—that's repentance—and by faith believe that Jesus is the Son of God, who loved us, paid the price for our sins on Calvary's cross, shed His blood and died, was buried, and was raised to life on the third day.

Prior to A.D. 312, Christianity was outlawed, and its followers persecuted. Historian Bruce L. Shelly in his book *Church History in Plain Language* says:

> Prior to Constantine's conversion, the church consisted of convinced believers. Now many came who were politically ambitious, religiously disinterested, and still half-rooted in paganism. This threatened to produce shallowness and permeation by pagan superstitions, but also the secularization and misuse of religion for political purposes." Shelly goes on to say, "Whatever Constantine's motive for adopting the Christian faith, the result was a decline in Christian commitment. The stalwart believers whom Diocletian killed were replaced by a mixture of half-converted pagans. Once Christians had laid down their lives for the truth; now they slaughtered each other to secure the prizes of the church.

Apostles Creed: Belief in the Virgin Birth, Trinity, Deity of Christ, the Resurrection

Before Constantine, the term "catholic," according to Shelly, was first used in the second century by Ignatius, who was Bishop of Antioch. The term was used to describe the "universal" Christian Church, which was the "spiritual vision" of Christ's Great Commission to spread the gospel message to all nations. Although not likely written by the apostles, the original Apostles' Creed, which first appeared in the second century, reflects the very essence and nature of the preaching of the apostles, and thus Christianity, in the first century.

Apostles' Creed

I believe in God, the Father almighty,
creator of heaven and earth,
I believe in Jesus Christ, God's only Son, our Lord,
who was conceived by the Holy Spirit,
born of the Virgin Mary,
suffered under Pontius Pilot,
was crucified, died, and was buried;
He descended to the dead.
On the third day He rose again;
He ascended into heaven,
He is seated at the right hand of the Father,
and He will come to judge the living and the dead.

I believe in the Holy Spirit,
the holy catholic (universal) Church,
the communion of saints,
the forgiveness of sins,
the resurrection of the body,
and the life everlasting. Amen.

By A.D. 380 Emperor Theodosius made belief in Roman Catholic Christianity, which had become the official religion of the entire Roman Empire, a matter of imperial command as opposed to the response of a repentant heart to the converting message of Christ's Gospel. Now non-Roman Catholics were persecuted, much as Christians were before the reign of Constantine (A.D. 312–337).

"Gradually, through the neglect of the Scriptures and the ignorance of the people, more and more man-made traditions were introduced into the Roman Catholic Church. Many of the pagan temples were taken over by the church and re-dedicated as Catholic cathedrals and churches. There remained, however, some groups small in numbers, who maintained the Christian faith in reasonable purity over the centuries, usually in more isolated places like northern Italy" (see *Church History in Plain Language*—pg. 230).

Protestantism: A Return to the Faith of the Apostles

In addition to Martin Luther, all the Reformers, including Calvin, Knox, and Zwingli among others, vehemently attacked the ignorance and superstition that had become such a large part of the Catholic Church beliefs, and like the apostles they gave the people a worship service in their own language with preaching based on the Word of God. Protestantism, therefore, was not a new religion but a return to the faith of the early church. It was Catholicism purified, with all the man-made traditions that it had collected during the Middle Ages thrown out. It was literally a back-to-the-Bible movement, a return to Apostolic Christianity.

It is clear from the Bible that Catholics and anyone else can be saved from eternal damnation if they repent of their sins, accept the Good News of the gospel message and live it, and accept the Jesus of the Bible as their personal Savior. The real question that all professing Christians must ask; are they really worshiping the Jesus of the Gospel, or are they being presented a different gospel and a different Jesus? As Paul said, "*My fear is that, just as the serpent seduced Eve by his cunning, your thoughts may be corrupted and you may fall away from your sincere and complete devotion to Christ. I say this because, when someone comes preaching another Jesus than the one we preached, or when you receive a different spirit than the one you have received, or a gospel other than the gospel you accepted, you seem to endure it quite well*" (2 Corinthians 11:3, 4).

Catholicism: A "Speculative and Mystical Theology"

Catholic author Karl Keating in his book *Catholicism and Fundamentalism* admits that there is a migration of Catholics into Fundamentalism, but very few Fundamentalists migrating into Roman Catholicism. This is true in spite of a massive Catholic parochial school system and Catholic colleges, that often have Catholic children under their influence from the first grade through college. On March 7, 2008, in response to a then recent Pew Survey on Religion, Father Roger J. Landry, a pastor in New Bedford, MA said, "It behooves Catholics and the Catholic Church to understand and address why approximately one-third of baptized Catholics leave the Church?" The Pew survey documents that of those who leave, 56 percent do so to join another church.

EWTN Television and Radio Networks put a major emphasis on encouraging and inviting former Catholics back into the fold of the Catholic Church through programs such as: *Journey Home, Catholics Come Home, Called to Communion, and Catholic Answers Live*, in addition to other broadcasts. Karl Keating is founder and senior Fellow at *Catholic Answers*, reportedly the country's largest apologetics and evangelization organization.

There appears to be a real attraction among many Catholics exposed to the simplicity of the Gospel message of traditional Evangelical Christianity, as opposed to the complex religious system of Catholicism that Keating refers to as "Speculative and Mystical Theology." This begins to make some sense when you compare Protestant Christianity to Catholicism, when you get beyond the Apostles Creed, which all Christians believe.

Basic Protestant Beliefs: Preach the Gospel, baptize, and celebrate Communion.

Basic Catholic Beliefs: The Mass, Priesthood, Transubstantiation, Purgatory, Prayers to the Saints, Prayers to the Dead, Prayers to Mary, The Papacy, Papal Infallibility, Infant Baptism, Celibacy, The Rosary, Stations of the Cross, Indulgencies, Confession, The Immaculate Conception, The Assumption of the Virgin Mary, Mary's Perpetual Virginity, exaltation of Mary, Mary as Mediatrix, Mary as Mother of God, Fatima, Lourdes, Guadalupe, The Apocrypha, Relics, The Scapular, The Blessed Sacrament, Images, Statues, One True Church Doctrine, Catholic Parochial School System, Holy Communion, Holy Water, Limbo, The Crucifix, Annulments, Tradition equal with Scripture, etc.

The primary answer to Keating's observation about the growth of Fundamentalism is that today's Catholics have greater access to the Bible than they had in past generations. Today, many Catholics belong to Bible studies both inside and outside the Catholic Church, which was unheard of in the 1950s. Catholics today are more open to making their own decisions about what the Bible teaches as opposed to what they are required to believe by their church. A Pew Research Survey, released by AP on November 13, 2014, reporting on the decline of Catholics in Latin America; from over 90 percent of the population in the 1960s, to 69 percent in 2014 and reported that the most common reason given by those that left Catholicism was that they wanted a more personal connection with God.

Hispanics Are Changing America's Religious Demographics

The *Wall Street Journal* reports: "Since the 1990s the Roman Catholic Church in the U.S. has seen Hispanics, many of them arrivals in a massive immigration wave, help bolster its shrinking ranks. The study released Wednesday (5/7/14) by Pew, a nonpartisan think tank, suggests a religious churning in the fast growing population group, the country's second largest. The share of Hispanics who are Catholic has been declining for at least the past few decades, Pew said, but from 2010 to 2013 it fell 12 percentage points to 55 percent, the study found. Nearly one in four Hispanic adults in the U.S. are now former Catholics, based on responses to Pew's poll, and a growing share identify as religiously unaffiliated or Protestant. The trends mirror what has been occurring in Mexico, Brazil, and other Latin American countries.

"To be sure, though the percentage of Hispanics who identify as Catholics in the U.S. has been falling, Latinos still account for an increasingly large share of all U.S. Catholics—about one-third in 2013—thanks to the growth of the Latino population. Hispanics account for about 17 percent of the U.S. population, up from 12 percent at the turn of the century."

The *Wall Street Journal* continues, "'If such trends continue, a day could come when a majority of Catholics in the U.S. will be Hispanic even if the majority of Hispanics might no longer be Catholic,' said Alan Cooperman, Pew's religion-research director" (The WSJ, May 8, 2014).

Other demographic trends that do not bode well for the Catholic Church in America going forward include: the decline of priests from fifty-seven thousand to thirty-eight thousand (down 35 percent) from 1965 to 2014, a 56 percent decline in graduate-level seminarians over the same fifty year period, a staggering 636 percent increase in parishes without a resident priest (from 549 to 3,496), a 72 percent decline in religious sisters, a 49 percent decline in Catholic elementary schools, and the fact that those attending Mass in any given week fell from 55 percent of Catholics in 1965 to 24 percent in 2014 (Georgetown University – CARA).

Evangelicals and Catholics Together: The Christian Mission in the Third Millennium

In the Catholic Church it is believed that grace is received from the sacraments of the Catholic Church, which include Baptism, Eucharist, Penance, Confirmation, Holy Matrimony, Holy Orders, and Extreme Unction. In Evangelical Christianity, grace is received when one is saved through an act of faith in Jesus Christ. A clear presentation of the Gospel message must precede true saving faith, which requires evangelism. "*But how shall they call on Him whom they have not believed? And how can they believe unless they have heard of Him? And how can they hear unless there is someone to preach*" (Romans 10:14)?

In the mid-1990s an effort was made to bridge the gap between Protestant Evangelicals and Roman Catholics. A group of notable Roman Catholic and evangelical leaders got together and published a document entitled, *Evangelicals and Catholics Together: The Christian Mission in the Third Millennium*. The document (ECT) supported the idea of Catholics and evangelicals working together, based on the notion that both evangelicals and Catholics are brothers in Christ, and should find common ground.

In the end, while there were many areas of common ground where these Catholic and evangelical leaders could agree, or at least have an open discussion, there were serious impediments to trying to bridge the theological divide between Catholics and Protestant Evangelicals.

The primary impediment to cooperation between Catholics and evangelicals was best expressed by Dr. John MacArthur, as reported by author Iain Murray, in his book about MacArthur. In that book Murray writes:

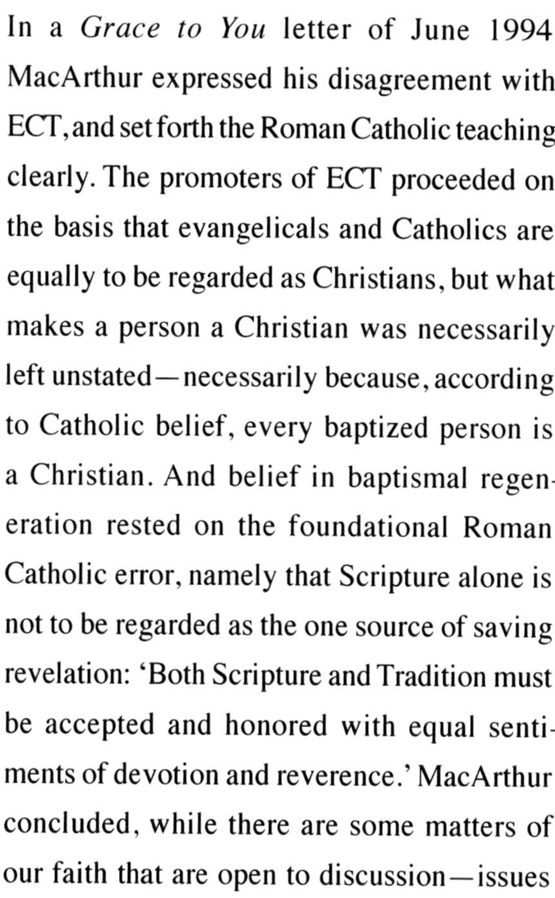

> In a *Grace to You* letter of June 1994, MacArthur expressed his disagreement with ECT, and set forth the Roman Catholic teaching clearly. The promoters of ECT proceeded on the basis that evangelicals and Catholics are equally to be regarded as Christians, but what makes a person a Christian was necessarily left unstated—necessarily because, according to Catholic belief, every baptized person is a Christian. And belief in baptismal regeneration rested on the foundational Roman Catholic error, namely that Scripture alone is not to be regarded as the one source of saving revelation: 'Both Scripture and Tradition must be accepted and honored with equal sentiments of devotion and reverence.' MacArthur concluded, while there are some matters of our faith that are open to discussion—issues

that many godly men disagree on—the means of salvation is not one of them.

Most Protestants believe that many Catholics are true Christians, based on the simple gospel requirement to believe that Jesus Christ is the Son of God, as given in John 3:16, "*Yes, God so loved the world that He gave His only Son, that whoever believes in Him may not die but may have eternal life.*" Still, it is difficult for some Protestants to accept Catholicism itself as true Christianity because of their belief that true Christianity is based on the biblical Gospel with nothing added. A biblical Christian believes in the full sufficiency of Scripture for his salvation, as supported by passages such as 2 Timothy 3:15–16: "*Likewise, from your infancy you have known the sacred Scriptures, the source of the wisdom which through faith in Jesus Christ leads to salvation. All Scripture is inspired of God and is useful for teaching—for reproof, correction, and training in holiness so that the man of God may be fully competent and equipped for every good work.*"

We read in the Scriptures, "*Now that we have been justified by faith, we are at peace with God through our Lord Jesus Christ*" (Romans 5:1). And further in Scriptures, "*Is it because you observe the law or because you have faith in what you heard that God lavishes the Spirit on you and works wonders in your midst? Consider the case of Abraham:*

he 'believed God, and it was credited to him as justice'" (Galatians 3:5–6).

In Catholicism There Are Many Additional Traditions Required for Salvation

To be a Catholic in good standing, one must believe in the official traditions and teachings of the Catholic Church, many of which are in conflict with God's Word in the Scriptures. Important Catholic traditions must be believed to be a practicing Catholic, beliefs like baptismal regeneration, justification by faith plus works, salvation can be lost, that membership in the Catholic Church is necessary for salvation, purification by purgatory, Christ's death on the cross was not fully sufficient to paid the full price for sin, and many more.

Additionally, the Catholic Catechism teaches that Catholics must also keep the Ten Commandments to attain salvation: "The Council of Trent teaches that the Ten Commandments are obligatory for Christians and that the justified man is still bound to keep them; the Second Vatican Council confirms: 'The bishops, successors of the apostles, receive from the Lord . . . the mission of teaching all peoples, and of preaching the Gospel to every creature, so that all men may attain salvation through faith, Baptism, and the observance of the Commandments" (CCC para. 2068). Trying to keep the Ten Commandments as a prerequisite for salvation is yet another example of the similarity of Catholicism to ancient Israel prior to A.D. 70.

Christians Believers Are under the New Covenant, Embodied in Jesus Christ

It is clear from the Old Testament that the Ten Commandments are the Old Covenant established by God with Israel: "*Then the Lord said to Moses, 'Write down these words for in accordance with them I have made a covenant with you and with Israel.' So Moses stayed there with the Lord for forty days and forty nights, without eating any food or drinking any water, and he wrote on the tablets the words of the covenant, the ten commandments*" (Exodus 34:27–28).

We know from the New Testament that Christ came bringing the New Covenant, thereby making the Old Covenant obsolete: "*If that first covenant had been faultless, there would have been no place for a second one. But God, finding fault with them, says: 'Days are coming, says the Lord, when I will make a new covenant with the house of Israel and with the house of Judah. It will not be like the covenant I made with their fathers the day I took them by the hand to lead them forth from the from the land of Egypt; for they broke my covenant and I grew weary of them says the Lord . . . I will place my laws in their minds and I will write them upon their hearts . . . I will forgive their evildoing, and their sins I will remember no more.' When he says, 'a new covenant,' he declares the first one obsolete. And what has become obsolete and has grown old is close to disappearing*" (Hebrews 8:7–13).

By its nature, the Covenant of the Law (Ten Commandments) was primarily external, but the New Covenant is internal, written on men's hearts. When a sinner repents and accepts Christ, they pass from being accountable under the Old Covenant (Ten Commandments) to Christ's New Covenant, which is now written on their hearts by the Holy Spirit who comes to dwell in them. The unredeemed, continue to be under the death sentence of the Law, or the Ten Commandments, which man being a sinner can never keep.

This is the very reason that the apostle Paul, can write in Romans, "*There is no condemnation now for those who are in Christ Jesus. The law of the spirit, the spirit of life in Christ Jesus, has freed you from the law of sin and death . . . Then God sent his Son in the likeness of sinful flesh as a sin offering, thereby condemning sin in the flesh, so that the just demands of the law might be fulfilled in us who live not according to the flesh, but according to the spirit*" (Romans 8:1–4).

Some might define Catholicism as a cult, but this label would be wrong since the Roman Catholic Church has always professed belief in the first century Christian creeds. As mentioned before, these early Christian creeds—the virgin birth, the Trinity, the Deity of Christ, and the Resurrection of Christ—are what historically distinguished the cults and false religions from Christianity, so we must conclude that the

Catholic Church professes Christianity. Like the reformers, the Catholic Church confesses these beliefs, as distinct from Mormons, Jehovah's witnesses, Hindus, Buddhists, Muslims, Jews, and others.

The Bible teaches that we are saved by grace through faith as written in Ephesians 2:8: "*I repeat, it is owing to His favor that salvation is yours through faith. This is not your own doing, it is God's gift.*" This truth of salvation by faith and not works is also verified in Galatians 2:16, "*Nevertheless, knowing that a man is not justified by legal observance but by faith in Jesus Christ, we too have believed in Him in order to be justified by faith in Christ, not by observance of the law; for by works of the law no one will be justified.*"

The Roman Catholic Church officially teaches that man is condemned if he believes that he can be saved by faith alone. The Catholic Church's Council of Trent (1545–1563), declared at the Sixth Session, Canon 9: "If anyone says that the sinner is justified by faith alone, meaning that nothing else is required to cooperate in order to obtain the grace of justification, and that is not in any way necessary that he be prepared and disposed by the action of his own will, let him be anathema (condemned)."

Both of the above views on justification, faith alone, and faith plus works, cannot be believed by the same person simultaneously. Faith will lead to good works, but good works do not lead to faith. One should conclude that the Word of God must take precedence over man-made tradition; therefore any Catholic, Protestant, or other Christian that holds to the biblical view as expressed in Ephesians 2:8–9, and lives by that truth, is a true Christian regardless of denomination, or non-denomination. To emphatically show that salvation is by faith alone, requiring nothing else, the apostle Paul writes, "*But when a man does nothing (no works), yet believes in Him who justifies the sinful, his faith is credited as justice*" (Romans 4:5). Many other Scripture verses confirm this truth of salvation by faith alone: Romans 5:1; Romans 11:6; Galatians 3:5–6; Romans 3:28–30; Romans 9:30; Romans 10:4, and Galatians 2:21, among others.

IX

God's Plan for Man's Salvation

What is God's plan for man's salvation? What must we do to become a member of this Body of Christ, which is the authentic, One True Church? It is simple: we must repent of our sins and believe (have faith) in the Jesus Christ of the Scriptures! This belief must be a life-changing experience from the heart and not just an intellectual acknowledgment and recognition of Christ. This heart-changing experience has nothing to do with joining a church denomination or any physical church; rather, it is a personal relationship with Christ whereby our very nature is changed, and we begin to live the Good News of the Gospel message:

For if you confess with your lips that Jesus is Lord, and believe in your heart That God raised Him from the dead you will be saved. Faith in the heart leads to justification, confession

> *on the lips to Salvation. . . . .Everyone who calls on the name of the Lord will be saved* (Romans 10:9–10, 13).

The Catholic Church teaches that God's plan of salvation is a process that does not begin with justification but rather ends in justification once all sins have been purged in purgatory (CCC para. 1030, 1031). This is a continuous process whereby Catholics are justified, then lose that justification when they commit a serious (mortal) sin, and then regain justification again after confessing their sin and receiving absolution from a priest, and to repeat this process until death. Philippians 2:12 is often used by Catholics to justify this Catholic plan of salvation, as the apostle Paul writes, "*So then, my dearly beloved, obedient as always to my urging, work with anxious concern to achieve your salvation, not only when I happen to be with you but all the more now that I am absent*."

God does not make mistakes, according to the Bible: ". . . *those He called He also justified, and those He justified He in turn glorified*" (Romans 8:30). Justification removes all penalty of sin the moment we declare faith in Jesus Christ, right from the very beginning. We are, then and there justified and declared righteous in God's eyes, through Christ's death and resurrection. In the above passage in Philippians, Paul is referring to the believer's responsibility for active pursuit of obedience in the process of sanctification. It is clear from many verses in the Bible that we are first justified for salvation by faith (past tense), but we are currently being sanctified, and we will surely be glorified in the future. This is the same process of experiencing salvation that Paul is referring to in 1 Corinthians 1:18: "*The message of the cross is complete absurdity to those who are headed for ruin, but to us who are experiencing salvation* (justification, sanctification, and glorification) *it is the power of God.*"

"*Nevertheless, knowing that a man is not justified by legal observance but by faith in Jesus Christ, we too have believed in Him in order to be justified* (past tense) *by faith in Christ, not by observance of the law; for by works of the law no one will be justified*" (Galatians 2:16).

God's Plan for Salvation Requires More Than an Intellectual Knowledge of Christ

To have faith that Jesus is Lord means more than just acknowledging that Jesus is Lord, more than just saying that Jesus is God. Even demons know that God is the sovereign of the universe. Confessing Jesus as Lord is expressing verbally, before others, your deep personal conviction that Jesus is your Master and the Ruler of your life. You must also believe in your heart that God raised Jesus from the dead, thereby fulfilling the sacrifice for all your sins. This is the only way we can truly conquer death!

"*The reason why Christ died for sins once for all, the just man for the sake of the unjust, was that He might lead you to* God" (1 Peter 3:18).

"*I repeat, it is owing to His favor that Salvation is yours through Faith. This is not your own doing, it is God's gift; neither is it a reward for anything you have accomplished, so let no one pride himself on it*" (Ephesians 2:8–9).

"*Because Scripture saw in advance that God's way of justifying the Gentiles would be through faith*" (Galatians 3:8).

We Cannot Earn Our Salvation

The Catholic Church teaches that good works are required for salvation. In (CCC para. 1821) we read, ". . . each one of us should hope, with the grace of God, to preserve 'to the end' and to obtain the joy of heaven, as God's eternal reward for the good works accomplished with the grace of Christ." The American Heritage Dictionary defines "work" as: "Physical or mental effort or activity toward the production or accomplishment of something; toil; labor. Further the AHD defines "works" in a theological context as: "Moral or righteous acts or deeds: *salvation by faith rather than works.*" It is clear from these definitions and Scripture itself (Ephesians 2:8-9;

Galatians 2:16), that "faith" itself is not defined as a work, as some might suggest.

The Bible says that our salvation is God's doing, not our own. The Bible is clear that we cannot earn our salvation. God has to bring our dead hearts to life, and He has to give sight to our blindness. God has to give understanding to our darkened minds. God must first give us the desire to seek Him before we acquire faith. Salvation is a miracle of God!

Catholic apologists often use the flowing two Bible verses as a "one-two-punch" in trying to show that salvation can actually be lost by not doing good works:

First, *"If you forgive the faults of others, your heavenly Father will forgive you yours. If you do not forgive others, neither will your Father forgive you"* (Matthew 6:14-15). This verse does not suggest that God will withdraw justification (salvation) from those who have already received the free pardon He extends to all believers. Forgiveness in that sense – a permanent and complete acquittal from the guilt and ultimate penalty of sin – belongs to all who are in Christ (see John 5:24; Romans 8:1; Ephesians 1:7). Scripture, however, also teaches that God chastens His children who disobey" (see Hebrews 12:5-70).

Secondly, *"When He will repay every man for what he has done: eternal life to those who strive for glory, honor, and immortality by patiently doing right; wrath and fury to those who selfishly disobey the truth and obey wickedness"* (Romans 2:6-8). Although Scripture everywhere teaches that salvation is not on the basis of works, it consistently teaches that God's judgment is always on the basis of a person's deeds. Paul describes the deeds of two distinct groups: the redeemed and the unredeemed. In these verses the deeds of the redeemed are not the basis of their salvation but the evidence of it. They are not perfect and are prone to sin, but there is undeniable evidence of righteousness in their lives" (see James 2:14-20).

We read in Romans that Abraham was justified by faith, not works; *"What then, shall we say of Abraham, our ancestor according to the flesh? Certainly if Abraham was justified by his deeds he has grounds for boasting, but not in God's view; for what does Scripture say* (see Genesis15:6)? *Abraham believed in God, and it was credited to him as justice"* (Romans 4:1-3).

We read in Romans, *"But when a man does nothing, yet believes in Him who justifies the sinful, his faith is credited as justice"* (Romans 4:5).

We read in Romans, *"Now that we have been justified by faith, we are at peace with God through our Lord Jesus Christ"* (Romans 5:1).

We read in Romans, *"For we hold that a man is justified by faith apart from the observance of the law"* (Romans 3:28).

We read in Titus, *"He saved us; not because of any righteous deeds we had done, but because of His mercy. He saved us through the baptism of new birth and renewal by the Holy Spirit"* (Titus 3:5).

We read in Thessalonians, "*God has not destined us for wrath, but for acquiring Salvation through our Lord Jesus Christ*" (1 Thessalonians 5:9).

We read in Ephesians, "*I repeat, it is owing to His favor that salvation is yours through faith. This is not your own doing, it is God's gift*" (Ephesians 2:8–9).

It is clear from the above Bible verses that man is justified (saved) in God's eyes by faith alone, through God's grace. This does not mean that he is justified in man's eyes by faith alone, because man cannot know what is in another man's heart. Man can only judge a person by the good works he observes. The problem is that those good works observed may not be the reflection of saving grace, and therefore worthless in God's eyes. Good works, regardless of their nature, cannot in and of themselves lead a person to salvation, but good works are indeed the fruit of salvation in a believer's life (see Ephesians 2:10).

There are many stories historically of the mafia in both the United States and Italy building churches, caring for widows and orphans, going to church each Sunday, and doing many other good deeds. These good works, as wonderful as they might be, could never erase the evil done in the daily lives of these crime families, and could never gain for them eternal salvation, regardless of how great the deeds, without full repentance and turning from a life of sin and crime. On the other hand a believer will demonstrate fruits of goodness in their lives, as a direct result of their faith and salvation. To say that it is necessary for salvation to have faith plus good works, saying that one cannot be saved by faith alone, is not biblical as is demonstrated by the many passages above. We are saved by faith alone, which then leads to good works, a very important distinction.

Many people who call themselves Christian never go to church while others claim that you can lose your very salvation if you willfully miss a Sunday church service. The truth is that church attendance neither saves you nor condemns you. What condemns people is their refusal to repent of their sins and accept God's divine plan for their life, which can only be found in the Bible. A believer who holds the Bible as their only source of authority is free to worship in any local church, regardless of the denomination, as long as that church teaches the authentic gospel of Christ. We know from Acts that the early churches were local and nondenominational (Acts 14:23, 27; 20:17, 28).

The Holy Spirit immediately places all people who put their faith in Jesus Christ into one united spiritual body, the Church, of which Christ is the head. The primary expression of the Church on earth is in autonomous local congregations of baptized believers. The primary purpose of the local Church is to glorify God by taking the gospel to the entire world and by building its members in Christ likeness through the instruction of God's Word, fellowship, service, worship, and prayer. Just as Christ associated with tax collectors and prostitutes, expect to find sinners (wheat and tares) in any local church.

The Gospel Plan of Salvation in a Nutshell

God's marvelous plan for man's salvation is beautifully summarized in the most quoted verses in all of Scripture, John 3:16– 18: "*Yes, God so loved the world that He gave His only Son, that whoever believes in Him may not die but may have eternal life. God did not send the Son into the world to condemn the world, but that the world might be saved through Him. Whoever believes in Him avoids condemnation, but whoever does not believe is already condemned for not believing in the name of God's only Son.*"

In these verses we find the parallel truths of God's divine sovereign love for the world, so much so that He freely gave His only Son, desiring that all might be saved. Yet, His sovereignty decides who will be saved, and who will not. God requires man's participation (free will), which is man's personal responsibility to believe (have faith) in His Son, Jesus Christ. This dichotomy, of God's sovereignty and man's free will is counterintuitive to man's reasoning but is clearly God's twin truth, based on Scripture.

In Matthew 11:27, we see that Jesus had received all authority and sovereignty from the Father, and Christ must do and give everything for man's salvation. "*Everything has been given over to Me by My Father. No one knows the Son but the Father, and no one knows the Father but the Son—and anyone to whom the Son wishes to reveal to him.*" Immediately, in Matthew 11:28, we see the contrast between God's sovereignty and man's role in salvation to come humbly, and to come in faith, believing. "*Come to Me, all you who are weary and find life burdensome, and I will refresh you.*" Finite minds cannot fully comprehend the truth that divine sovereign grace and faith are inseparable in salvation. God sovereignly provides salvation through His grace, which includes the fact that man must submit himself by believing in Christ before that salvation becomes effective.

We read in Romans 9:13–16, "*It is just as Scripture says, 'I have loved Jacob and hated Esau.' What are we to say, then? That God is unjust? Not at all! He says to Moses, 'I will show mercy to whomever I choose; I will have pity on whomever I wish.' So it is not a question of man's willing or doing, but of God's mercy.*" And Romans 19:18 reads, "*So He has mercy on whom He desires, and He hardens whom He desires*" (NASB). The principle of divine election does not mean that God is unfair in His dealings with men. Rather, He reveals in this way that the gift of faith is the enactment of His mercy.

Divine Sovereignty and Human Responsibility Are Compatible in God's Economy

In a *Grace Partners* letter of September 2013, Pastor-Teacher John MacArthur writes, "Scripture teaches both divine sovereignty and human responsibility side by side, without ever being apologetic or evasive. What's more, what we believe about those doctrines really does matter. It affects our love and reverence for God, how we think about and engage in evangelism, and how we deal with the heartache of loved ones who reject the Lord and die in their sins."

Sadly, most of the world's population has rejected God, by rejecting His Son, Jesus Christ. Eighty-five percent of the world's population identifies with some religion or relationship with God, or a god, that ultimately promises eternal salvation or an afterlife in one form or another. The remaining fifteen percent of the world's population claim to be atheists, agnostic, or secular humanists of one variety or another.

"*Whoever believes in the Son has life eternal. Whoever disobeys the Son will not see life, but must endure the wrath of God*" (John 3:36).

According to God's plan, salvation can only be achieved by those who believe that Jesus Christ is God made man, who died to save man from his sin, was resurrected from the dead on the third day after his crucifixion, and today sits at the right-hand of the Father, waiting for His Second Coming.

"*This Son is the reflection of the Father's glory, the exact representation of the Father's being, and He sustains all things by His powerful Word. When He had cleansed us from our sins, He took His seat at the right hand of the Majesty in heaven*" (Hebrews 1:3).

Nearly one-third (32 percent) of the world's population, 2.1 billion people, profess to be Christian, claim to believe in the Christian biblical plan of salvation, and would have some expectation of heaven as believers in Jesus Christ (85 percent of American Christians). Unfortunately, the remaining almost five billion people on planet earth having presumably rejected Christ as the Son of God, are disqualified for eternal salvation, and are sadly doomed to eternal damnation. This result would seem harsh to many, who naturally think of God as a loving and all merciful deity.

Surprisingly, a detailed examination of Scripture seems to indicate that many, if not most, of the 2.1 million professing Christians, also will not inherit eternal salvation because of their lack of genuine faith. As we noted earlier, Christ puts true salvation into proper context in chapter seven of the Book of Matthew 7:13–14, "*Enter through the narrow gate. The gate that leads to damnation is wide, the road is clear, and many choose to travel it. But how narrow is the gate that leads to life, how rough the road, and how few there are who find it!*" The narrow gate represents true salvation, which is by faith, through God's grace, but it is not easy, and requires knowledge of truth, repentance, submission to Christ as Lord, and a willingness to obey His will and His Word. The wide gate includes all religions of the world and self-righteousness, with no single way, but it leads to hell, not heaven. Most dictionaries define "Few" as "more than one, but not many."

The Coming of the Son of Man Will Repeat What Happened in Noah's Time

When we read the following verses from Matthew, the picture of salvation becomes even clearer. We read in Matthew 7:21–23, "*None of those who cry out, 'Lord, Lord.' Will enter the kingdom of God but only the one who does the will of My Father in heaven. When that day comes, many will plead with Me, 'Lord, Lord, have we not prophesied in your name? Have we not exorcised demons by its power? Did we not do many miracles in your name as well?' Then I will declare to them solemnly, I never knew you. Out of My sight, you evildoers!*" These people who professed to be followers of Christ were claiming to have done remarkable signs and wonders. In fact their entire confidence was in these works—further proof that these works, spectacular as they might have appeared, could not have been authentic. Scripture is telling us that no one so deprived of genuine faith could possibly produce true works. A bad tree cannot bear good fruit (Matthew 7:18).

We read the following, in the Book of Matthew, concerning the final days, "*Because of the increase of evil, the love of most will grow cold*" (Matthew 24:12). John MacArthur comments, "Evil will multiply so rapidly and unashamedly that many people who are initially drawn to the gospel will turn away from it because of the multiplied enticements of sin. The lawlessness will be diabolically aggressive and unabashed. Rather than trying to hide their sins, people will flaunt them, and such gross evil will draw many people, including some professed believers, away from whatever interest in the things of God they may once have had."

These above passages taken together should be a sobering thought for all of those who are professing Christians anticipating eternal salvation. Christ appears to be painting a very narrow and demanding window of salvation opportunity for even those who think they are believers but who will find out on judgment day that their professed Christianity was unacceptable to God. These passages would indicate that, apart from the nearly five billion unbelievers of the world today that appear to reject Christ outright, many, if not most, of the professing Christians of the world will be shocked on judgment day to find out that they also were not included in the few who enter through the narrow gate into eternity in Christ's presence.

If we consider the relatively few people living today, who will likely be saved by the implications of Matthew chapters seven and twenty-four, we might also think this outcome harsh for a loving and merciful God. But then we would do well to read the account of Noah and the great flood in Genesis. We read in Genesis 6:5–6, "*When the Lord saw how great was man's wicked-ness on earth, and how no desire that his heart conceived was ever anything but evil, He regretted that He had made man on the earth, and His heart was grieved.*" Then reading on in Genesis 6:11–13, "*In the eyes of God the earth was corrupt and full of lawlessness. When God saw how corrupt the earth had become, since all mortals led depraved lives on earth, He said to Noah* (who had found favor in the eyes of the Lord): '*I have decided to put an end to all mortals on earth; the earth is full of lawlessness because of them. So I will destroy them and all life on earth.*" God then told Noah to build an ark of gopher wood, and that only he and his family would escape the worldwide flood that He would bring on mankind and all living creatures on land and in the water.

Many Are Called but Few Are Chosen

Mathematician Tom Pickett, using sophisticated mathematical models, and taking into consideration long life-spans (Methuselah died at 969 yrs.), family size, and the 1,656 years between Adam and Eve and the great flood, was able to estimate a reasonable pre-flood world population of between 5 and 17 billion people, depending on the average number of children used in his model. So it is reasonably estimated, using his model, that the world population at the time of the great flood was likely around 10 billion people, or three billion people more than today.

We read in Genesis 7:12, 13, "*For forty days and forty nights heavy rain poured down on the earth. On the precise day named, Noah and his sons Shem, Ham, Japheth, and Noah's wife, and the three wives of Noah's sons entered the ark.*" Genesis 7:21 reads, "*All creatures that stirred on earth perished: birds, cattle, wild animals, and all that swarmed on the earth, as well as all mankind.*" So we know that God spared only eight human beings out of a total world population of around ten billion people. So, as we watch the continuing moral decay in our world today, we should not be surprised that, "*the gate is small and the way is narrow that leads to eternal life, and few will find it.*"

Speaking of the great Tribulation yet to come, a further reading of Matthew Chapter 24 confirms that our world will experience the same moral decay that lead to the great flood. "*Indeed, you will be hated by all nations on my account. Many will falter then, betraying and hating one another. False prophets will arise in great numbers to mislead many*" (Matthew 24:10–11). Because of God's mercy, and because of Christ's Church and the Holy Spirit, the growth of evil has been restrained from full-bloom for some four thousand years since the great flood, but like in the days of Noah, man continues on a relentless path of his own self destruction and sinfulness, by rejecting Christ's continuing call for repentance. "*The coming of the Son of Man will repeat what happened in Noah's time*" (Matthew 24:37). Interestingly, predictions are that the world's population will once again reach 10 billion people in the year 2062 (Worldometers).

In a message preached in 1960, Billy Graham said, "The Bible teaches us that demonic activity has always been prominent in history, but as the age draws to a close, it will be intensified. God is permitting, under certain restrictions, Satan and his myriad demon helpers to work at this unholy ambition."

The moral decline of the world we are living in today has been greatly accelerated in the last fifty years by an ever advancing technology that allows the evils of pornography, murder, terrorism, violence, greed, idolatry, potential massive nuclear destruction, and all forms of perversion and immorality to permeate the Internet and our homes exposing our families to evils unimagined in past generations. We know from the Bible, as Billy Graham said in 1960, that it will get even worse as time goes on. It appears that the world's population is on schedule to become just as evil as Noah's generation.

Finally, The biblical plan of salvation is simple in that Jesus Christ and Him crucified is the only way to heaven through faith in His shed blood for our sins. He is the only way one can truly know God the Father and experience His love and grace; sin separates man from God, but God, who is rich in mercy, has sent His only begotten Son that whosoever believes in Him shall live and not die!

If you are unsure where you will go when you die, consider what God's Word tells us in the Scriptures:

First, God loves you! "*Yes, God so loved the world that He gave His only Son, that whoever believes in Him may not die but have eternal life.*" (John 3:16)

Second, Man is a sinner, and sin has separated him from God!—"*Yet there is no man on earth so just as to do good and never sin*" (Eccl. 7:20); "*All men have sinned and are deprived of the glory of God. All men are now undeservedly justified by the gift of God, through the redemption wrought in Christ Jesus. Through His blood, God made Him the means of expiation for all who believe*" (Romans 3:23).

Third, Jesus Christ and what He accomplished at the cross 2,000 years ago is the only remedy for sin—"*The reason why Christ died for sins once for all, the just man for the sake of the unjust, was that He might lead you to God" (1 Peter 3:18); "There is no salvation in anyone else, for there is no other name in the whole world given to men by which we are to be saved*" (Acts 4:12).

<u>Fourth</u>, You must repent (turn from sin) and by faith, receive Jesus Christ as your personal Lord and Savior ever trusting in His accomplished work on the cross for salvation and walking in victory once one is born again—Jesus calls this experience the "new birth." He told Nicodemus, "*I solemnly assure you, no one can see the reign of God unless he is begotten from above*" (John 3:3); "*Any who did accept Him He empowered to become children of God*" (John 1:12). This is your invitation to receive the Lord Jesus Christ as your personal Savior.

Salvation is about God's sovereign will! God chose the "elect" (those that would believe) before the beginning of time, in eternity past, by His sovereign will. God sent His only begotten Son to earth to pay the ultimate and necessary price for every sin that the "elect" would ever commit, so that God's will would be realized. Christ paid this price "in full" in a single sacrificial act on Calvary two thousand years ago, and through His death the entire work of redemption was brought to completion. "It is finished," (John 19:30). Although God is sovereign, He works through faith, so that a person must believe in Jesus as the Messiah and Son of God who alone offers the only way to salvation. Even this faith, however, is a gift of God. Our High Priest, Jesus Christ, gave absolution to each believer for all the sins they would ever commit, even before they were born, so there is now no need of further absolution from sin for those in Christ Jesus.

Through the atoning work of Christ, the believer's sins are forgiven, his relationship with God is restored, and eternal life with God in glory is assured.

The biblical doctrine of election is presented throughout the New Testament, (John 17:2; John 15:16-19; Acts 13:48; Romans 8:29-33; Ephesians 1:3-6; 2 Thessalonians 2:13; Titus 1:1; 1 Peter 1:2).

X

SUMMARY

In *The One True Church* the author has made an effort to take a balanced approach to examining Catholic doctrines: using the Catechism of the Catholic Church, the Catholic Bible, Catholic authors, and other Catholic resources while using the Bible, Bible commentaries, religious history, evangelical authors, and personal experience in an attempt to gain a perspective on Catholic traditions and history from a layperson's point of view.

We know from Holy Scriptures that the only way man can have salvation and eternal life is through repenting of his sins and believing that Jesus Christ is God (Mark 1:15; Romans 10:9–10, 13; John 3:16; John 14:6). This is a personal decision that must be made by each individual. Joining a particular church or being baptized into a family that espouses a particular religious doctrine cannot save us. Those individuals that belong to a cult or false religions that do not accept Jesus Christ as God, or that believe that Jesus was a good man, a good teacher, a prophet, or that all religions worship the same god, are excluded from eternal life according to God's Word. This means that those who believe and practice the tenets of Judaism, Hinduism, Buddhism, Islam, Mormonism, Jehovah's Witnesses, Scientology, atheism, agnosticism, secularism, and others are excluded from God's promises, according to God's own Word in the Scriptures. True believers are called to walk in the light and have nothing to do with the works of darkness.

All denominations that say that they believe in the early Christian creeds: the virgin birth, that Jesus Christ is God, the Second Person of the Holy Trinity, and believe in Christ's death and resurrection, are professing to be Christian. Many denominational and nondenominational churches today may be in some degree of apostasy and need to repent and reform, just as we read about in the Book of Revelation. By definition, the Roman Catholic Church and every other Christian church today, regardless of denomination, or non-denomination, falls somewhere in the spectrum from faithful to Christ's teachings to full apostasy and abandonment of faith in Christ and His teachings. Christ praised the church at Ephesus for their hard work for Him and for not tolerating evil men, or false apostles, and for hating the deeds of the Nicolaitans. He, however, rebuked them for leaving their first love, which was their original strong singular love of Christ and His teachings. Christ's command to the Church at Ephesus was, "*Keep firmly in mind the heights from which you have fallen. Repent, and return to your former deeds. If you do not repent I will come to you and remove your lampstand from its place.*" (Rev. 2:5).

To the Church in Sardis Christ said, "*But you have a few people in Sardis who have not soiled their garments; and they will walk with Me in white, for they are worthy*" (Rev. 3:4). The Sardis church needed to go back to their original belief in the teachings of the apostles. By A.D.100, Sardis had Paul's letters and the rest of the New Testament had been written, but they had left the truths of Scripture, and the church was spiritually dead. Christ's command to the church at Sardis was, "*Wake up and strengthen the things that remain, which are about to die . . . So remember what you have received and heard; and keep it, and repent. Therefore if you do not wake up, I will come like a thief, and you will not know at what hour I will come to you*" (Rev. 3:2–3—NASB).

The One True Church Is neither Catholic nor Protestant

The One True Church was not any of these local physical churches, not even the Philadelphia and Smyrna churches, which were not in apostasy. Instead, The One True Church was comprised of the true believers in each of these seven churches, whether few or many. This has been true throughout church history even until today, as the Body of Christ includes all the true believers, regardless of church denomination or level of apostasy of the local church fellowship they might attend.

It must be concluded from the irrefutable evidence presented by God's own Scriptures that The One True Church cannot be the Roman Catholic or Protestant churches, or any other church institution or denomination. The clear prerequisite for The One True Church is stated in Matthew 16:18, where Christ declares, "*. . . and on this rock I will build My church, and the jaws of death (gates of hell-NASB) shall not prevail against it.*"

Both Roman Catholic and Protestant institutional church history is replete with evidence of corruption and the evil of demonic activity prevailing against these religious institutions. What could not have been overpowered by Satan, however, were (and are) those individual true believers who, from the beginning were God's elect who obeyed His Word, resisted evil, and continued with a singular focus on Christ and the gospel.

The First Century Christian Church Was Foremost a Gospel Preaching Church

Over the past 1,700 years the Roman Catholic Church has worked very hard to try to close the historical gap between A.D. 33, when Christ established His church at Pentecost, and A.D. 313 when Constantine legalized Christianity in the Holy Roman Empire, which was the genesis of the Roman Catholic

Church of today. If you believe Roman Catholic tradition, you would have to believe that the apostles were traveling around Galilee, Judea, Samaria, Italy, and Greece in the first century celebrating Mass, believing in Transubstantiation, confessing their sins to a priest for absolution, baptizing infants, praying to Mary and the saints, and believing in purgatory. This extrapolated picture of the first century Christian Church simply did not exist historically.

As mentioned earlier, the Catholic Church believes in the Trinity, the deity of Christ, the virgin birth, and the death and resurrection of Jesus Christ, which are found in the early creeds of the Apostolic Church. The Catholic Church, however, also requires that Catholics, in order to be saved, must believe in purgatory, indulgences, good works are necessary for salvation, the sacraments, the infallibility of the pope and the Magisterium of the Catholic Church, the Assumption of the Virgin Mary into heaven, the Immaculate Conception, and membership in the Catholic Church. None of these additional Catholic Church traditional requirements are recorded in Scripture as prerequisites for salvation.

These traditions of men represent a different gospel than the one recorded in the Scriptures. The most famous Scripture verse in the Bible, and the one that many describe as the simple Christian Gospel in a nutshell has only one requirement: "*Yes, God so loved the world that He gave His only Son, that whosoever believes in Him may not die but may have eternal life*" (John 3:16).

The danger in believing in all of these additional traditions for our salvation is the truth that each additional requirement leads us further into apostasy and further away from our first love, which should be Christ alone. The professing Christian who lives his life trying to fulfill and satisfy all of the above complex traditional requirements of the Catholic Church loses the joy of salvation of the true believer, who is focused on the simplicity of the gospel message that Jesus offers to every repentant sinner.

There are two churches! One is apostolic and includes all believers that have been baptized of the Holy Spirit, into the Body of Christ, and the other is an apostate church made up of those who name Christ, but believe and follow a false gospel.

Jesus Promises the Believer: Assurance of Salvation, Forgiveness, His Righteousness

The Lord Jesus' basic promises to the repentant sinner are foreign to Catholic theology and to most Catholics. The Magisterium of the Roman Catholic Church condemns those individuals that accept the below three basic promises of Christ Himself to the repentant sinner. This puts Catholic parishioners, who truly believe they are members of The One True Church, in the awkward position of committing spiritual suicide should they deny the authority of the Catholic Church's teachings on these promises of Christ; should they decide to follow the Bible and not their church:

First, the **absolute assurance of salvation** is promised to the new believer at the moment of their acceptance of Jesus Christ as their savior:

The apostle Paul says, *there is no condemnation now for those who are in Christ Jesus*" (Romans 8:1). "*The law of the Spirit, the Spirit of life in Christ Jesus, has freed you from the law of sin and death*" (Romans 8:2). "*We know that God makes all things work together for the good of those who love God and are called according to His decree*" (Romans 8:28). Paul is saying that the believer is "invincible," as "all things work together for good," includes everything that happens to the believer, both the good and the bad. This does not mean that sin is good, but only that God will even turn the believer's sin into good for the believer, because it has been predetermined by God that the believer will be glorified.

If these verses were not enough to make Paul's point absolutely clear about the security of the believer, he finishes the eighth chapter of Romans with the following flurry of verses to leave no doubt about the assurance of salvation: "*Those whom He foreknew He predestined to share the image of His Son . . . Those He predestined He likewise called; those He called He also justified; and those He justified He in turn glorified. . . . If God is for us who can be against us? . . . <u>For I am certain</u>* (emphasis added) *that neither death nor life, neither angels nor principalities, neither the present nor the future, nor powers, neither height nor depth nor any other* *creature, will be able to separate you from the love of God that comes to us in Christ Jesus, our Lord*" (Romans :31–39).

Second, the new believer receives **the complete forgiveness of sins**:

The apostle John writes, "*But if we acknowledge our sins, He who is just can be trusted to forgive our sins and cleanse us from every wrong*" (1 John 1:9). Luke writes, "*Therefore, reform your lives! Turn to God, that your sins may be wiped away*" (Acts 3:19)! And again Luke writes, "*To Him all the prophets testify, saying that everyone who believes in Him has forgiveness of sins through His name*" (Acts 10:43). The prophet Isaiah writes, "*It is I, who wipe out, for My own sake, your offenses; your sins I remember no more*" (Isaiah 45:25). Not only does God completely forgive us our sins, but He also does not remember our sins anymore! The writer of Psalms confirms Isaiah's truth: "*As far as the east is from the west, so far has He put our transgressions from us*" (Psalms 103:12). Peter writes, "*In His own body He brought your sins to the cross, so that all of us, dead to sin, could live in accord with God's will*" (1 Peter 2:24).

Third, Christ gives the sinner, the new believer, **full credit for His perfect righteousness:**

Timothy writes, "*From now on a merited crown awaits me; on that Day the Lord, just judge that He is, will award it to me—and not only to me, but to all that have looked for*

His appearing with eager longing" (2 Timothy 4:8). Matthew writes, "*Blessed are they who hunger for and thirst for holiness (righteousness); they shall have their fill*" (Matthew 5:6). Again Matthew writes, "*Seek first His kingship over you, His way of holiness* (righteousness)*, and all these things will be given you besides*" (Matthew 6:33). Paul writes, "*For our sakes God made Him who did not know sin, to be sin, so that in Him we might become the very holiness* (righteousness) *of God*" (2 Corinthians 5:21). At the moment of our acceptance of Christ as our Master and Savior, Christ took the filthy rags of our sinfulness, and He freely gave us His perfect righteousness, crediting to our account that holiness/righteousness/justification, which He earned for us at Calvary.

As hymnist Edward Mote penned in 1834 in his popular hymn, The Solid Rock, "My Hope is built on nothing less than Jesus' blood and righteousness. I dare not trust The sweetest frame, but wholly lean on Jesus' name."

Catholics, however, are taught that they are committing the "sin of presumption" if they say that they have eternal life, rather than believing what Christ promises in the Bible. Catholics depend on indulgences, penance, and purgatory to pay for the residual punishment that they believe is still due for their sin, even after death, rather than trusting Jesus for His promise of complete forgiveness of their sins. And, rather than receiving Christ's promised imputed perfect righteousness as a free gift, Catholics try to earn their righteousness (holiness) through good works and the sacraments, as taught by the Catholic Church.

In God's economy the temporal punishment or reparations due for sins of the believer are just that, temporal punishment that must be paid in this life, not in eternal life. If a man commits murder, and truly repents, then God will forgive him for eternity. There is nothing he can do in this life or the next to restore the life he has taken. Society, however, will demand a temporal punishment, that may require his own life or prison. Most sin has a temporal price to pay emotionally or materialistically, and for the believer the price is paid in this life, but for the unbeliever that price is both paid in this life and in the life to come. Sins that may not be considered a crime legally, still often result in temporal punishment for the sinner in broken trust, broken relationships, embarrassment, guilt, retribution, injury, heart break, disease, and much more. God's forgiveness for sin is eternal, complete, and so perfect that God no longer even remembers our sin. God does not demand additional payment in eternity for the sins that He has already forgiven. The thief on the cross, who repented of his sins and was rewarded in paradise the very day that he died, demonstrates this truth.

Most of the Traditions of the Catholic Church Began as a Concept or a Practice

Most of the doctrines of the Catholic Church began as a concept, or a practice that became popular with the laity or the clergy, sometimes over hundreds of years, and were eventually in such widespread practice that the Catholic Church decided to officially make the concept a binding doctrine for the entire church, separate and apart from authorization from Scripture. For example, around A.D. 250, Cyprian, bishop of Carthage, likely celebrated the first Mass. The Mass developed gradually; it was celebrated once a week, then three or four times a week, and finally in the fifth century every day, but it was only made obligatory for Catholics to attend Mass in the eleventh century. Purgatory began evolving after the time of Augustine (circa A.D. 430), but it was only made an official doctrine of the Catholic Church at the Council of Florence in 1439. Statues first appeared in churches after A.D. 335, began developing in earnest in the sixth century, and were finally officially authorized by the Council of Nicaea in 787.

Sprinkling water for baptism was first practiced in A.D. 250, but only dogmatized at the Council of Ravenna in 1311 after being forbidden by the Synod of Cologne in 1280. Confession to a priest was first introduced in the fifth century on a voluntary basis but made compulsory in 1215. The Immaculate Conception was first established by Pope

Sixtus IV in 1476 but dogmatized by Pope Pius IX in 1854. Celibacy was introduced in 800 but only made compulsory at the Lateran Councils of 1123 and 1139. Infallibility of the pope was only introduced for a vote, and made a binding belief for all Catholics at Vatican I in 1870 (not A.D. 33). Indulgences were approved by the Council of Clermont in 1095. The concept of the Assumption of Mary into heaven has been around since the fourth century but was only made an infallible doctrine of the Catholic Church in 1950, by Pope Pius XII, and Transubstantiation was only dogmatized at the Fourth Lateran Council in 1215.

We often hear Catholics say, "Unlike Protestants, we have "The fullness of the faith" in the Catholic Church—The Blessed Mother, purgatory, the Mass, the sacrament of Penance, Indulgences, and much more." In the case of our salvation, however, "more" is often"less." Catholics need to be good Bereans, and test each of these Catholic doctrines against God's Word in the Scriptures: "*Each day they studied the Scriptures to see whether these things were so*" (Acts 17:11). The Old Testament prophet, Jeremiah warns us against trusting in human beings for our guidance, as opposed to the Lord's guidance in His Word: "*Thus says the Lord: Cursed is the man who trusts in human beings, who seeks his strength in flesh, whose heart turns away from the Lord*" (Jeremiah 17:5).

The Catholic Church has evolved over the centuries into a complex institutional religious system with many dogmas, doctrines, rituals, rules, and traditions requiring a nine-hundred page catechism to define for Catholics what they must believe to be a Catholic in good standing in their church. Many Catholics have little knowledge of the details in this catechism (1994), which was revised including numerous changes from earlier catechisms. In contrast, the Bible never changes, and has stood the test of time in it's truth, accuracy, and simplicity in presenting the "Good News" to all who have "the eyes to see and the ears to hear."

The Dangers of Being Politically Correct

From the many man-made traditions of Catholicism mentioned above that are not supported by Scripture to the knowing or unknowing worship, by definition, of the Virgin Mary to the worship of the Eucharist (CCC 1378) by practicing Catholics, we must conclude that the Roman Catholic Church today has evolved over the centuries into a Christian Church that is in apostasy and in need of repentance and reform. In today's politically correct world, where many Christians are uncomfortable pointing out error, they often fail to present the simple gospel of salvation through Christ alone to their Catholic family and friends for fear of hurting their feelings or being called intolerant, legalistic, judgmental, or worse, in spite of the fact that their friends' and loved one's very salvation might be at stake.

Christ had little tolerance for those that opposed His teaching, by teaching traditions that were not His, as we can read in the Scriptures: "*Woe to you scribes and Pharisees, you frauds! You shut the doors of the kingdom of God in men's faces, neither entering yourselves nor admitting those who are trying to enter*" (Matthew 23:13).

Many Protestant churches of all denominations and those that are nondenominational are also in apostasy and in need of repentance and reform. Many now famous television ministers are preaching a health, wealth, and prosperity false gospel that is found nowhere in the pages of Scripture. These false preachers are proud, deceptive, and spiritually destructive, and focus on man's happiness, comfort, and prosperity in this life. They extract money from poor souls with false promises of happiness, healing, and wealth. Paul describes a totally different Christian ministry in 2 Corinthians 6:4–6: ". . . *in that all that we do we strive to present ourselves as ministers of God acting with patient endurance amid trials, difficulties, distresses, beatings, imprisonments, and riots; as men familiar with hard work, sleepless nights, and fastings; conducting ourselves with innocence, knowledge and patience, in the Holy Spirit, in sincere love*." Further, Paul writing to Timothy tells us that, "*Anyone who wants to live a godly life in Christ Jesus can expect to be persecuted*" (2 Timothy 3:12).

Many mainline Protestant churches, of all stripes, are also preaching a compromised gospel, or no gospel at all, even though they also claim to believe in the Apostles' Creed of the first-century church. Many have moved away from preaching a gospel of repentance verse by verse and are engaged in storytelling, ritual, motivational messages, videos, political correctness, good works for the sake of good works, entertainment in various forms, and a gospel message that has been compromised by conforming to the world mentally and materialistically.

In the May 2014 *Decision Magazine*, Billy Graham said, "It seems that some diabolical mastermind is running the affairs of this world and that his chief objective is to brainwash Christians and to get them to conform to this world."

The message from the Book of Revelation is clear to all churches in apostasy: Repent and open up to Christ before the Day of Judgment comes. All churches that claim to be Christian should be modeling themselves after the churches at Smyrna and Philadelphia, which kept their focus on Christ and Christ alone.

Christian Apostasy Is Ubiquitous in Today's Growing Secular World

Many of the professing Christian churches, regardless of, whether Catholic or Protestant, are clearly at some level of apostasy, having left the simple gospel of Christ: "*But I hold this against you, though: you have turned aside from your early love*" (Revelation 2:4). In the Book of Revelation the angel of the Lord told the apostle John that the church in Ephesus' passion and fervor for Christ had become cold, mechanical orthodoxy. Their doctrinal and moral purity, their undiminished zeal for the truth, and their disciplined service were no substitute for the love of Christ that they had forsaken.

Christ tells us in the parable of the wheat and tares that from the very beginning until the end of time even those churches that have not lost their singular focus on Christ, will still have unbelievers (tares or weeds) in their midst:

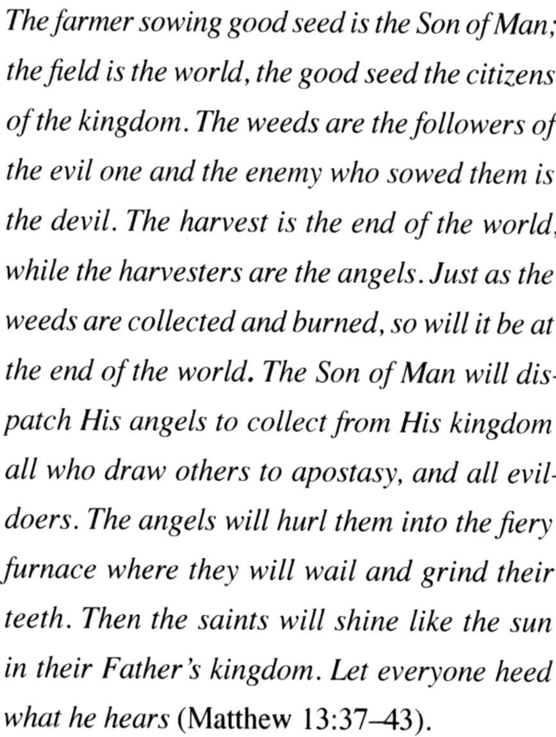

The farmer sowing good seed is the Son of Man; the field is the world, the good seed the citizens of the kingdom. The weeds are the followers of the evil one and the enemy who sowed them is the devil. The harvest is the end of the world, while the harvesters are the angels. Just as the weeds are collected and burned, so will it be at the end of the world. The Son of Man will dispatch His angels to collect from His kingdom all who draw others to apostasy, and all evildoers. The angels will hurl them into the fiery furnace where they will wail and grind their teeth. Then the saints will shine like the sun in their Father's kingdom. Let everyone heed what he hears (Matthew 13:37–43).

Wheat (good seed—true believers) and weeds (unbelievers) must exist side by side, breathing the same air, enjoying the same sunshine and rain, eating in the same restaurants, attending the same schools, working in the same offices and plants, living in the same towns and cities, and often attending the same churches, until He comes again.

Finally, the Bible describes, and history records, that from the beginning of the Church Age to our present time, Satan and his cohorts have infiltrated the institutional church. In A.D. 51, Paul writes of false teachers misleading many at the church in Thessalonica. In A.D. 55, Paul had to discipline the church at Corinth for allowing false teachers into their church encouraging licentiousness among the congregation. Paul instructed the Corinthians to remove the wicked from among them. We know that the five churches in Asia Minor that John describes in the Book of Revelation were in some level of apostasy by A.D. 100. History has recorded much about the scandals, evil, and corruption in the institutional church from the Middle Ages even until now.

Clearly, Satan and the gates of hell have prevailed against these institutional churches since the first century, but Satan and the gates of hell could never prevail against God's elect, the Body of Christ, as Christ tells us in Matthew 16:18. This leaves man with only one infallible resource and authority by which to guide his life, the Holy Bible. It is clear from Scripture that The One True Church, is not the Roman Catholic Church, or any institution but rather all the true believers that are members of all Christian Churches; whether they are few or many, only God knows. This reality should convince concerned Catholics to examine every Catholic doctrine against their Catholic Bible, as did the Bereans, *"to see if these things* (church doctrines) *are so."* Each Catholic must ultimately decide who they will trust for their eternal destiny. They must decide between trusting human tradition, even if taught by their church in the Catechism, or trusting Jesus and His infallible Word and teachings, found in their Catholic Bible. Clearly, the safest choice is to trust in Jesus Christ and the proven truth of Scripture.

The One True Church is comprised of all those believers that accepted, or will accept in the future, Christ as their Lord and Savior, during the Church Age, from the Book of Acts until the Second Coming. **All those who are worthy to be clothed in white will walk with the Lord.**

XI

CONCLUSION

As I pass my seventieth birthday, I sense that it is time to bring my over thirty-year journey of study to gain a biblical and historical perspective on Catholicism to its conclusion in the pages of this book. I feel certain that the main beneficiary in this exercise was meant to be, and has been, me. I felt a spiritual encouragement and grew in my knowledge and understanding of Catholicism and the Bible over the years. That being said, however, scores of people have come to me over that period of time, wanting to hear "my story," which gave me an opportunity to place in their hands a copy of my manuscript in its many stages of development. If I can now help others who might be on a similar journey of searching for truth, by sharing my learning experiences with them, I will consider myself richly blessed.

The Author Is a Simple Layman, Not a Scholar or a Theologian

I was not a scholar when I began this project, and I am certainly not a scholar today as I write the concluding pages. I have been humbled over these years as some of my research presented in previous manuscript editions, eleven in all, had errors that I subsequently found and corrected; nevertheless the exercise left me with the reality that nothing is perfect, and certainly this work does not meet God's perfection either. I have done my best, however, with a rather limited intellect and a layman's limited skill-set to be as accurate as possible when presenting the historical facts, as I have learned them over the years; and in presenting the associated biblical truths while prayerfully studying them over time. I have diligently given the reader direct quotes from the Catholic Bible, to give many a comfort zone, but they must determine for themselves if the commentary associated with those passages ring true for them.

Realizing my own bias in coming out of Catholicism thirty-two years ago, I have attempted to report the facts as I found them along the way, and as I have written them in *The One True Church* from the introduction on page one to the summary near the end. I have attempted, to the best of my ability, to give the facts and expert commentary on the facts, while trying to keep my personal editorial commentary to a healthy minimum. Nevertheless, I am sure that I have failed along the way to always properly assign emphasis to certain points due to human failings on my part. The reader will have to make those judgment calls for themselves.

God Has Looked Beyond My Faults and Has Seen My Needs

Over these many years God has looked beyond my faults and has seen my needs and has unfailingly met them. I give God the glory! My journey has taught me the unbelievable power of prayer. I prayed from my earliest memories as a child, but my prayers have grown from an intellectual exercise, delivering rote prayers that were rather pedestrian, to a daily devotion to prayer realizing that God has promised to answer our prayers in His precious Word if we pray according to His will. The prerequisite for answered prayer is a relationship with Jesus that is honest and trustworthy; one where we are not trying to deceive God or ourselves. We must be believers and not pretenders. It is clear from Scripture that God wants to have a constant dialogue with His elect, through His Son Jesus Christ. The most powerful form of worship is prayer!

The Bible is overflowing with directions for us on praying, encouragement to pray, and on the power of prayer:

"*You will receive all that you pray for, provided you have faith*" (Matthew 21:22).

"*If you, with all your sins, know how to give your children what is good, how much more will your heavenly Father give good things to anyone who asks Him*" (Matthew 7:11)!

"*He* (Christ) *told them a parable on the necessity of praying and not losing heart*" (Luke 18:1).

"*Pray perseveringly, be attentive to prayer, and pray in a spirit of thanksgiving*" (Colossians 4:2).

"*Present your needs to God in every form of prayer and in petitions full of gratitude*" (Philippians 4:6).

"*When I call, answer me, O my just God, you who relieve me when I am in distress; Have pity on me, and hear my prayer*" (Psalm 4:1)!

When Jesus overturned the money-changers in the temple He said, "*My house shall be called a house of prayer*" (Matthew 21:13).

As the years have gone by and as I have continued to pray for my Catholic family and friends, I have realized that many of those wonderful Catholics could teach all of us who claim the title of Christian to be better followers of Christ in how they serve the poor, the immigrant, the sick, the uneducated, and often how they treat each other. If many non-Catholic Christians only had the loyalty to the gospel of Jesus Christ that many Catholics have to their church, we would be seeing revival in the Christian Church in America today rather than a decline in membership and attendance in almost all denominations. Unfortunately, just being good and being loyal to an institution, even if it is one's church, is not good enough in God's perfect economy, as only Christ's perfect imputed righteousness can give us the perfection that is required for salvation, as a free gift, through God's grace, by our faith in Jesus Christ.

Catholic Church Takes Responsibility—Apologizes for Sins of the Past and Present

Over these thirty-plus years I have gone from discouragement over the prospects of the Catholic Church reforming to hope in seeing popes finally accept responsibility for the historical sins of the Catholic Church against Protestants, Jews, and others. Pope John Paul II, Pope Benedict XVI, and Pope Francis have all identified scandals and corruption in the church, and have apologized and accepted responsibility for the church, putting into place safeguards in the Catholic Church to try to prevent a repetition of these sins in the future, something their many predecessors over the centuries failed to do.

Pope Francis Named *Time* Magazine's Person of the Year

Time magazine selected Pope Francis as its Person of the Year for 2013, saying the Catholic Church's new leader has changed the perception of the institution in an extraordinary way in a short period of time. At the time, with less than a year as leader of the Catholic Church, Reuters reported, "Pope Francis has firmly established himself as an agent of change. Francis has already come under scathing criticism from a growing number of traditional Catholics for cracking down on a religious order that celebrates the old Latin Mass, having a more open view toward homosexual priests, and open hostility toward 'unfettered capitalism,' but Pope Francis denies being a Marxist (NBC News/Reuters 12/15/13).

A February 2015 Pew Research Poll indicated that Pope Francis' popularity continues to grow among Catholics and the general American population as a whole. Pope Francis received a 90% favorable rating among Catholics, which was up from 84% in March 2013. In the same poll Pope Francis received a 74% favorable rating among white mainline Protestants, which was up from 65% in March 2013, while white evangelical Protestants gave Pope Francis a 60% favorable rating, up from 59% in March 2013. Favorable ratings from other United States demographic groups in the Pew Poll included: Blacks 56%, Conservatives 67%, Liberals 74%, Hispanics 71%, Men 69%, Women 70%, Catholic Men 88%,

Catholic Women 91%, Hispanic Catholics 86%, Catholics attending weekly mass 95%, and Catholics attending weekly mass less often 86%.

Pope Francis and the Challenge of Catholic Reform

Pope Francis gets high marks from most people for being proactive on the scandals in the church, at the Vatican Bank, and on his humble lifestyle, which is characterized by his frugality. He rejected the luxurious papal apartment in the Vatican's Apostolic Palace to live in a small suite in a Vatican guesthouse, and he drives a Ford Focus, which he prefers over the traditional pope's Mercedes. He is clearly a champion of the downtrodden and poor, but it is uncertain how this compassion for the poor and weak, promoting a church that "is poor and for the poor," will play out in a Catholic Church today, which is recognized as one of the wealthiest institutions in the world.

Pope Francis in his early days as pontiff has shown boldness in many comments and actions, including skipping the centuries old customary Vatican process by bestowing sainthood—by decree—on Father Pierre Favre, a sixteenth-century Jesuit priest and by canonizing two popular popes together, foregoing many of the formalities applying to canonization. The kind of reform necessary to bring today's Catholic Church to a singular focus on Christ, however, will require the stature and boldness of a Pope Gregory the Great.

The real question is; can and will Pope Francis initiate the type of reform that brings the Catholic Church to a position of accepting non-Catholic Christians as equal brothers in Christ, and more importantly, can and will Pope Francis initiate the kind of significant reform of Catholic doctrines concerning "the means of salvation," that non-Catholic Christians can embrace Catholics as equal brothers in Christ, even though there may not be complete harmony on many minor issues that do not impact what the Bible teaches is necessary for salvation? This kind of significant reform within the Catholic Church would require repealing many of the major doctrines coming out of the Council of Trent in 1546.

Only time will tell, but many in the non-Catholic Christian world and the Catholic world are encouraged that Pope Francis, known as a reformer, is speaking out on some of these Catholic Church positions, signaling a dramatic shift in tone from the Vatican. Pope Francis said, "The church's pastoral ministry cannot be obsessed with the transmission of a disjointed multitude of doctrines to be imposed insistently . . . The church sometimes has locked itself up in small things, in small-minded rules" (*Dallas Morning News* 9/20/13).

At a traditional Christmas gathering of the Curia in Vatican City Pope Francis accused the Vatican Curia of living hypocritical lives (AP–December 23, 2014):

> Pope Francis issued a blistering indictment of the Vatican bureaucracy...accusing the cardinals, bishops, and priests who serve him of using their Vatican careers to grab power and wealth, of living 'hypocritical' double lives and forgetting that they're suppose to be joyful men of God.
>
> Francis turned the traditional, genteel exchange of Christmas greetings into a public dressing-down of the Curia, the central administration of the Holy See, which governs 1.2 billion-strong Catholic Church. He made clear that his plans for a radical reform of the structure of church power must be accompanied by an even more radical spiritual reform of the men involved.

God's Mercy toward Sinners Is Long-Suffering

Clearly, God never gives up on the sinner, and He never gives up on institutional Christianity in our local churches and denominations. All He asks is for sinners, whether individuals or churches in apostasy, to repent of their error. It is up to the wheat (true believers) in all denominations and churches to insist that the true gospel be preached, or those Christians should seek a fellowship of believers that are following the gospel according to Jesus. The many "tares" sitting in all church pews are lost, without the preaching of the true Word.

In the Book of Revelation, God told the churches in apostasy to repent. He gave them yet another opportunity to return to their first love, which is Christ. Since these churches are prototypes of churches today, God's mercy is available even today, as it was then. To the church at Ephesus, for example, the angel of the Lord told the apostle John to write this: "*Keep firmly in mind the heights from which you have fallen.* Repent and return to your former deeds. *If you do not repent I will come to you and remove your lampstand from its place*" (Revelation 2:5).

Even to the church at Laodicea, which was lukewarm towards God, God offered another chance to repent and get right with Him; the angel of the Lord instructed the apostle John to write, "*Whoever is dear to Me I reprove and chastise. Be earnest about it, therefore. Repent*" (Revelation 3:19)!

The Bible Is the Glue that Holds Christianity Together

I trust that the reader of this book will agree that the Bible is the only reliable resource that God has given us as our instruction manual on life, as I have attempted to prove and record in the pages of this book. It is clear from Scripture that The One True Church is the Body of Christ and not the Catholic Church or any other church or denomination. The glue that holds all members of the Body of Christ together, and therefore Christianity, is the Bible and only the Bible. Hence, it is necessary for every believer to test every tradition, doctrine, and dogma against the ultimate source of truth that God gives us in His Word, regardless of the specific teaching of one's local church or denomination. Again, as has been previously emphasized, the apostle Luke tells us that we must be like the Bereans: "*Each day they studied the Scriptures to see whether these things were so*" (Acts 17:11).

Christian Churches That Are Teaching Error Need to Repent and Reform

Can any reasonable person look at our world today and not be alarmed by the wars in the world, rumors of war, terrorism, nuclear proliferation, blatant immorality, Internet pornography, crime, political corruption, business corruption, poor church attendance, weak leaders, drug addiction, legalization of harmful drugs, legalized homosexuality, abortion, a compromised gospel being preached in many churches and on television and not think that we might very well be in those final days spoken of by the apostle Paul?

The apostle Paul warns us of false teachers in Second Timothy when he writes:

> *Do not forget this: there will be terrible times in the last days. Men will be lovers of self and money, proud, arrogant, abusive, disobedient to their parents, ungrateful, profane, inhuman, implacable, slanderous, licentious, brutal, hating the good. They will be treacherous, reckless, pompous, lovers of pleasure rather than God as they make a pretense of religion but negate its power. Stay clear of them* (2 Timothy 3:1–5).

Paul then challenges Timothy, and by extension each of us today, when he writes "*I charge you to preach the word, to stay with this task whether convenient or inconvenient—correcting, reproving, appealing—constantly teaching and never losing patience. For the time will come when people will not tolerate sound doctrine, but will follow their own desires, will surround themselves with teachers who tickle their ears. They will stop listening to the truth and will wander off to fables*" (2 Timothy 4:2–4).

Is it not time for the Body of Christ to rise up in all our institutional churches—whether Catholic, Baptist, Presbyterian, Methodist, Pentecostal, Independents, or others— and demand and pray for repentance and reform in our churches and a return to the preaching of the gospel according to Jesus

Christ? If over 70 percent of the seven churches spoken of in the Book of Revelation were already in some level of apostasy by A.D. 100; would we not be foolish to think that most of our Christian Churches today, after two-thousand years of man's influence, are not in some level of apostasy, and need to return to their first love, that of Jesus Christ?

In these last days, I am but a small voice asking all members of the Body of Christ in all churches to pray daily that Pope Francis will significantly reform the Catholic Church and that Protestant leaders will reform and all return to preaching the gospel of Jesus Christ so that all who call themselves Christian can unite under Christ for the battle that surely will come to all that name His name as Savior? It is only the fervent prayers of God's elect that can change our churches into beacons of hope for the hopeless, and that can bring revival to our rapidly deteriorating churches and world. Prayer is the most powerful weapon in the arsenal of the saints and the ultimate form of worship of our matchless God. *"You will receive all that you pray for, provided you have faith*" (Matthew 21:22).

We can be sure that God will reward all sinners and all churches that repent, even at this late hour, if they will only come, but the danger is that sinners and churches will wait too long, and it will be too late . . . time is passing, the lost are dying, **"and Night Cometh, when no man can work!"**

Appendix A

The Solid Rock

"My hope is built on nothing less than Jesus' blood and righteousness. I dare not trust the sweetest frame, But wholly lean on Jesus' name.

Refrain: On Christ, the Solid Rock, I stand, all other ground is sinking sand; all other ground is sinking sand.

When darkness veils His lovely face, I rest on His unchanging grace. In every high and stormy gale, my anchor holds within the veil.

Refrain: On Christ, the Solid Rock, I stand, all other ground is sinking sand; all other ground is sinking sand.

When He shall come with trumpet sound, O may I then in Him be Found. Dressed in His righteousness alone, Fault-less to stand before the throne."

Refrain: On Christ, the Solid Rock, I stand, all other ground is sinking Sand; all other ground is sinking sand."

Edward Mote

Appendix B

Important Dates in the History of the Roman Catholic Church

312 Roman Emperor Constantine converts to Christianity, but is only baptized in 337

313 Constantine's Edict of Milan makes Christianity legal in the Roman Empire

380 Emperor Theodosius defines "Roman Catholic Christianity" as the state church

382 Catholic Church authorized Jerome to translate the Bible into Latin (The Vulgate)

394 The Mass now celebrated daily in Africa, but on Sundays only in other regions

431 Exaltation of Mary as "Mother of God"—Council of Ephesus

787 Second Council of Nicaea authorized use of images and relics for the first time

927 Beginning of College of Cardinals (Electors of the Pope)

1000 Mass made obligatory for all parishioners (approx. date)

1090 Rosary introduced by Peter the Hermit and later popularized by St. Dominic

1096 Indulgences were approved by the Council of Clermont

1123 Priestly Celibacy made compulsory at Lateran Councils of 1123 and 1139

1198 The Inquisition or "Holy Office" instituted by pope Innocent III

1215 Transubstantiation proclaimed a doctrine at Fourth Lateran Council

1215 Confession to a priest made compulsory once a year at Fourth Lateran Council

1220 Adoration of the host decreed by Pope Honorius III

1229 Possession of Bible by laymen prohibited by Council of Toulouse

1244 Heretics ordered sentenced by Council of Harbonne—"burned without pity"

1251 Scapular introduced by Simon Stock an English Monk

1302 Catholic Church declares that salvation requires a person to be subject to the pope

1302 Pope claims authority over every nation in the world—*Unam Sanctam*

1311 Sprinkling of water for baptism made an option by the Council of Ravenna

1431 Joan of Arc ordered burned at the stake by Pope Martin V

1439 Purgatory doctrine formalized at the Council of Florence, and at Trent (1546)

1439 Seven Sacraments of Catholic Church doctrine confirmed at Council of Florence

1531 Mary or an image of Mary appeared to Juan Diego at Guadalupe, Mexico

1545 Tradition declared of equal authority with Bible at Council of Trent

1546 Apocryphal books added to canon of Catholic Bible at Council of Trent

1546 The Mass is declared identical with the sacrifice of the cross at Council of Trent

1616 Galileo banned by the Catholic Church from teaching, speaking in public, writing

1816 Pope Pius VII condemned reading of the Bible

1834 650 years of Inquisition ends with abolishment of the Spanish Inquisition

1854 The Immaculate Conception was defined as a dogma of the Catholic Church

1858 Mary or an image of Mary appeared to Bernadette Soubirous at Lourdes, France

1870 Papal Infallibility declared to reside with the pope alone

1917 Mary or an image of Mary appeared to three children at Fatima in Portugal

1950 The Assumption of Mary made dogmatically infallible by Pope Pius XII

1962 Vatican II convened with theme of reconciliation with other denominations

1965 Mary proclaimed Mother of the Roman Catholic Church by Pope Paul VI

2007 Bishops announce priest abuse cases in U.S. since 1950 cost Church $2.3 Billion

2013 Pope Benedict XVI first pope to resign papacy since Gregory XII in 1415

2013 Cardinal Jorge Mario Bergoglio of Argentina, a reformer, named Pope Francis

Works Consulted

Blanchard, Paul. *American Freedom and Catholic Power* , 1949.

Boettner, Loraine. Dr. *Roman Catholicism.*

Bruce, F. F. *The Canon of Scripture*

Catholic Church. *The Catechism of the Council of Trent,* 1566.

De Courcy, Philip. *Standing Room Only. .*

De Liguori, Bishop Alphonse. *The Glories of Mary*. Nihil Obstat: Rev. Arthur J. Scanlan STD and Imprimatur: Patritius Cardinalis Hayes.

Gilles, Anthony E. *People of God, The History of Catholic Christianity*. Nilil Obstat: Rev. Lawrence Landini, O.F.M., et al.

Greenleaf, Simon. *The Testimony of the Evangelists.*

Hardon, John A., S.J. *The Q and A Catholic Catechism.*

Hurlbut, Jesse Lyman. *The Story of the Christian Church.*

Juris, Paul. *Blessed Mary.*

Keating, Karl. *Catholicism and Fundamentalism*. Nihil Obstat: Rev. Msgr. Joseph Pollard, S.T.D. and Imprimatur: Most Reverend Archbishop Roger Mahony.

Keating, Karl. *What Catholics Really Believe.*

Lisle, Jason. *How Do We Know the Bible is True.*

MacArthur, John, Dr. *The MacArthur New Testament Commentaries*

Manchester, William. *A World Lit Only By Fire.*

Pezzotta, Dr. Anthony. *Truth Encounter*

The New American Catholic Bible Nihil Obstat: Stephen J. Hardegen, O.F.M., S.S.L., Imprimatur: Patrick Cardinal O'Boyle, D.D. Archbishop of Washington.

Orlandis, Jose. *A Short History of the Catholic Church.*

Ratzinger, Joseph Cardinal. *Catechism of the Catholic Church.*

Schaff, Philip. *History of the Christian Church.*

Shelly, Bruce L. *Church History in Plain Language.*

Thomsett, Michael C. *The Inquisition: A History.*

Index

CPSIA information can be obtained at www.ICGtesting.com
Printed in the USA
LVOW11*0459100615

441842LV00001B/1/P